There Will Be No Rescue

Steve Aiken

www.soazcc.org

© 2007 by Steve Aiken.

All rights reserved. No part of this book may be reproduced, stored in a retrieval system or transmitted in any form or by any means without prior written permission of the copyright holder, except by a reviewer who may quote brief passages in a review in a newspaper, magazine or journal.

Second printing

Printed in the United States

*Then call on me when you are in trouble,
and I will rescue you...* **Psalm 50:15 NLT**

**Dedicated to:
Horatio Spafford
Roscoe Arbuckle
Richard Jewel
John Stoll
Joelle Ogletree
And all of those who have suffered "the pain."**

Table of Contents

Introduction

My scrapbook 8

Chapter

1. Flying solo…………………………………..19

2. The other date that will live in infamy………………41

3. Before a Fall, Always Pride……………………..64

4. False Charges…………………………………..77

5. From bad to worse……………………………...100

6. When will I learn?..116

7. You are not alone……………………………....126

8. Progressives – Liberals;
   a different religion…………………………………..140

9. Is society playing God?..153

10. The breaking process……………………………166

11. My Radio Show…………………………………179

12. Legally Whacked……………………………….186

13. Finding your way out……………………………211

14. The Caboose …………………………………...231

My autobiography, written for the "Christian" who may have strayed from Lord, and cannot find their way back. This evangelistic tool will also hold the interest of the "non-believer," from start to finish. For those who have been hurt or scarred in or by Christians, churches, or Christian organizations, this is *a must read for those who have fallen and can't get up!*

As a former police officer, bodyguard, D.C. lobbyist, and radio talk show host, I tell the story of my life with a self-help approach I hope, will encourage the reader.
From the pinnacle of success to absolute ruin and public scorn; from breaking my neck to coming back years later and winning a state racquetball championship; and from running one of the most heated congressional campaigns in the country, to losing almost everything in our lives again. I hold nothing back in sharing the biblical, life lessons, I have learned.

ATHEISTS PROCEED WITH CAUTION!

If you have ever been through a dramatic experience that caused you to lose faith, seemed to ruin your life, shattered your religious beliefs, or kept you from fellowship with others, this book is for you.

Perhaps you are at that desperate stage of having lost a loved one – a period in life where every waking moment is painful and depressing because of the loss you have suffered or the hurt that has been inflicted. Even sleep brings you no rest and you wake every morning only to have the darkness and depression come rushing in, reminding you again of the pain and emptiness you suffer this day.

Are you feeling abandoned by God, family, friends, and no one can bring you comfort? Have you been driven to anger or bitterness by your experiences?

Then this book is for you.

Learning that others have experienced similar events puts you miles ahead of the curve on your way to recovery. It does not matter what horrible thing or things may have happened to you that shipwrecked you emotionally; perhaps others ripped you off, tried to ruin you, broke your confidence, or lied to you. Maybe you're just miserable because all you see in church circles are hypocrites and phonies. Maybe you slipped back into an old, unhealthy habit or lifestyle.

No matter what happened to get you to this point, there are some common elements to all of these tragedies. When you learn these basic elements, you will gain strength to overcome your battles and crawl out of the darkness. With the help of the Lord and some of the teachings in this book, we will pray for your speedy return.

In God I will praise his word,
in God I have put my trust;
I will not fear what flesh can do unto me. **Psalm 56:4**

People are created in the image of God, and are composed of spirit, mind, and body.

Throughout this book, I use military metaphors. Although I never served in the military, I have had the pleasure of training and working with members of the Israeli Mossad, the United States Secret Service, the New Scotland Yard, and Navy Seals. I would not dare make light of the sacrifice and dedication of those who serve or served in the military. I use the analogies ONLY to allow the reader to picture the lessons being taught in a spiritual sense.

As a young man pinned down and eventually captured by the enemy – this is my story. This is the story of my eventual capture and subsequent escape from the enemy's camp, all done while I served (spiritually speaking) in the Army of God. Don't get me wrong, this is not an army that uses guns or bullets or bombs. This is an army that uses spiritual weapons that are mighty through God for the pulling down of strongholds. This is the true story of how in full-time Christian service I met people other people say they would "die to meet" – two presidents of the United States three different times, senators, congressmen, kings, movie stars.

You will also read about how my wife and I achieved "success" beyond our wildest dreams with a mission for homeless teenagers in the Philadelphia area. This eventually came crashing down around us, causing us to lose almost everything, a direct result of my mistakes, failures, and yes, sins!

My Scrapbook

*PHOTOS DO NOT REPRESENT ENDORSEMENTS

Former President George and Barbara Bush and I

"Guarding" Bob Dole

Former British Prime Minister Lady Margaret Thatcher, Dr. Tim LaHaye

John Ashcroft

Former Congressman JC Watts

Louis Freeh- FBI Director 1993-2001

* Former Congressman Tom Delay
* Modified photo

Christian Singer, Steve Green

Whitewater investigator, Ken Starr

Arizona Gubernatorial candidate, Don Goldwater, nephew of the late, great Barry Goldwater

Col. Oliver North

Bob Dole meeting Deborah for the first time

Me walking on stage with Bob Dole

Guarding Presidential Candidate, Alan Keyes

Rev. Billy Graham & Jack Kemp

Presidential candidate, Gary Bauer

Dr. Charles Stanley

Actor, James Sikking

Bay Buchanan, AZ State Rep. Russell Pearce, and Randy Graf
(*More about Randy Graf later*)

**This photo DOES represent an endorsement
Sarah, Deborah and Stephanie Aiken**

Later you'll read that while hosting the fastest growing radio talk show in Arizona and running the most hotly contested congressional campaign in the country, I lost it all again by no fault of my own. This forced me to apply the principles in this book and to be able to say by faith – *it is well with my soul!*

This book also captures the essence of my core beliefs, most of which became the foundation for my talk radio show in Tucson Arizona. Learn with me as I dissect things that utterly shattered my life while I deployed methods and ways I thought I was an expert in using. Re-live with me how after 17 years of "faithful" service to God, I almost died a slow spiritual death. This is by no means a justification of my wrongs, and it's not exactly a public confession. I write this book with the hope that you won't take the same wrong turns I did. I also hope that for those of you who feel trapped, this book will give you a road map to escape. I only wish someone had written something like this for me!

Chapter 1
FLYING SOLO

I once saw a movie called "The Rock." (*I know "Christians" are not supposed to go to the movies – if that's the worst thing you ever did in your life, this book is probably not for you!*) It's about a fictitious Marine Corps General who took over the island prison of Alcatraz. This highly decorated, most honorable general sought recognition for those under his command who had fallen in the service of their country. His men ran 'black ops,' a slang term for certain military missions that men are sometimes called upon to perform.

These secret missions are usually extremely sensitive and politically volatile in nature. If you remember the old "Mission Impossible" television show or even the more recent movies, there is a line that goes something like this: "*…as always, if you or any of your men are caught or captured, the Secretary will disavow any knowledge of your mission.*"

In other words, **YOU'RE ON YOUR OWN, PAL!**

In the beginning of the movie, as the credits are rolling, you hear a young lieutenant in Vietnam, trapped and pinned down behind enemy lines. Bombs are exploding; bullets are whizzing; sheer chaos can be heard over the crackling of the radio transmissions. The lieutenant cries out for help – ***"We can't hold out much longer, sir!"***

As the audio version of this scene plays out, a military funeral is shown at Arlington National Cemetery. A few seconds go by, and again, over the bombs bursting and the machine gun fire, this young lieutenant is heard to say: *"General Hummel you gotta get us out of here – NOW!"*

"………I won't let you down; I won't let you down son," is our fictitious general's response.

General Hummel is frantically trying to get his men help from other divisions.

"Damnit sir, how long do we have to wait? I lost 15 of my men already; they're lighting us up like a fire storm."

"This is General Hummel, you gotta get my men out of there NOW!"

"We don't have clearance to go behind enemy lines, sir," is the only response heard.

After a long pause, our young lieutenant resigns himself to the fact that help is not coming. *"They're not coming for us, are they, sir?"* are the last words we hear this brave young man say.

No, they are not! The quicker you learn that people – yes, even those who claim to be your friends – even if they claim to be "Christian"– will let you down, the quicker you are going to find yourself on the road to recovery.

Recovery from what? If you have never met my "commander in chief," Jesus Christ, then you need "recovery" from your sins. If you ever had something horrible happen to you, don't think that this terrible thing happened in a vacuum, for it did not. Others have been affected by your affliction. Others have been through what you are going through and I would hasten to say that to the police officer in Phoenix, Arizona, who had his face burned beyond recognition or the housewife whose children have all grown up and her husband left her for a younger woman. **Remember, no matter how bad things get for us, there is always someone whose situation is worse than yours.**

If these types of tragedies, or poor choices, have befallen you as God's way of getting your attention, then I suggest you do just that – **PAY ATTENTION**! Many have learned the "secret" of a happy & blessed life, IT IS POSSIBLE, regardless of the fact that we are all headed in the same direction. What comes after that, is what is REALLY important. The curse of death started in the book of Genesis, Chapter 2, Verse 17, and continues all the way through the Bible. Yes, I believe every word of the good book – the Bible. Contrary to some reports, the Bible has never been proven to be wrong. Not historically, not geographically and certainly not scientifically. In addition to that, the entire book and God's plan contained therein, make perfect sense to me.

    However, there is GOOD NEWS! We all go through tough times and times of personal growth. That's not to say God does not desire your happiness and joy down here on earth: He does. There are, however, certain immovable principles we all must face in our lives. As you'll read later in the book, I probably witnessed more death by the time I was 17 years old than most people see in a lifetime.

    You will also read how I once knew the Lord and served Him, and then fell into a life of drugs, alcohol, women, and violence. I am not saying I have all the answers to your problems; believe me, I don't. If you take the time to look past the wretchedness of the author, I promise you there are some "life lessons" I learned in the enemy's camp. I learned quickly that many people will let you down, disappoint you, or say stupid things that hurt you. Of course not all people will always let you down. In my case, and perhaps in yours, the Lord was teaching me – although I did not know it at the time – that He and HE alone is the only one coming behind enemy lines to rescue us!

If I make my bed in hell behold you are there.
Psalm 139:8b

The prophet Jeremiah wrote: *Thus saith the Lord; Cursed [miserable] be the man that trusteth in man, and maketh flesh his arm, and whose heart departeth from the LORD.* **Jeremiah 17:5**

footnote Matthew Henry put it this way: "Those that trust to their own righteousness and think they can do well enough without the grace of Christ, *make flesh their arm,* and their souls cannot prosper; they can neither produce the fruits of acceptable services to God nor reap the fruits of saving blessings from him; they dwell in a dry land."

Are you dwelling in a dry land today, a deserted place? Wondering where God is in the middle of the storm? Perhaps the most horrible circumstances you may be going through or have gone through? I sure was. I can't tell you how many times I became bitter with local pastors and Christians at the various churches I attended. For years I had thought these guys were my "friends." I spoke at their churches, they supported my ministry, we often broke bread together at their houses or mine – excuse my language, but where the hell are they now?

Like that young lieutenant, I was angry because they never sent a "rescue party." With very few exceptions – though there were some – nobody went behind enemy lines to try to pull my wife and me out of the worst spiritual firestorm we have ever gone through. But we made it out alive!

I mess things up – *when I do things my way, instead of God's!*

As much as I hate talking about myself, it's kind of hard to write a book about your life without doing so. Although this book is somewhat of an autobiography, I hope that those reading it will find strength for the battles ahead, especially for those who are reeling from the effects of a "shattered faith."

It's not biblical to say, but I don't consider myself to be that great a Christian. However, I have learned so much from my Christian experience, I feel I would be remiss if I did not share some of the life lessons I gained along the way. There are so many true stories to tell about my life, I hesitate to touch on many of them for fear of being labeled a braggart; however, I think it was Babe Ruth who said: "*It ain't braggin if it's true.*"

I'll briefly describe some of the highlights and lowlights. For instance, do you know anyone else who was an ambulance attendant and a police cadet at the ripe old age of 16 and saw more blood and gore by the time he was 17 than most people see in a life time? From innocent babies who died of crib death to bodies charred beyond recognition, train crashes, suicides, gun battles – like a lot of police and rescue squad members, I can honestly say I've seen it all. It started when I was 16 years old and I'm not sure it will stop even now that I'm 50+.

One hot summer day in 1974, I was hanging out at Volunteer Medical Service Corps (VMSC) headquarters, reading training manuals and waiting for 911 calls. As trainees in the Lansdale, Pennsylvania, department, my best friend at the time, Pete Alles, and I were given instructions that were very clear – we were allowed to ride on the ambulance as trainees/observers, but we had to clearly identify ourselves as trainees. That way, the ambulance driver would know to wait for another qualified medic to get on board before we left the station.

About all I knew of first aid at that stage of my life was basic bandage wraps I learned in Boy Scouts. When the call came in, it was a young child hit by a car in Hatfield Township. With pagers beeping and alarm bells ringing, all I knew to do was to open the huge bay garage door, start the ambulance, and wait for a qualified team to show. I was going on my very first emergency run – my mouth was dry and my knees were shaking. About 60 seconds later, a four wheel drive vehicle with flashing blue lights came screeching into the parking lot. Out rolled 6'2", 285 lbs., Wayne Sarver – as foreboding-looking as he was qualified. Mr. Sarver held the rank of lieutenant in the VMSC and was huffing to catch his breath as he approached the driver side door with me just standing there waiting for the rest of the crew.

"Get in" was all he said as he pointed at me and motioned toward the ambulance.

"I'm only an observer, I'm not qualified," I replied, as I had been instructed.

"Get the F*** in" was Wayne's only response.

I was 16 years old and jumped in the front seat at this gigantic man's command. We took off with lights and sirens blaring for the five minute ride to the scene of the accident. Over the two-way radio we heard: "3-4-5-2 police report a young boy is down and request you make it on the double."

Sarver barked at me to pick up the radio and say '10-4' – of course, I did.

We pulled up to the intersection of West 8th St. and Koffel Rd. Several police cars were already there. All I saw was a little seven year old boy lying on the street with a small, training wheel bicycle nearby. Wayne picked the child up and put him on the stretcher (not exactly medically recommended) and ordered me to the back of the ambulance with the boy for the five block ride to North Penn Hospital. I did what I was told and held the unconscious boy's hand, repeatedly telling him he would be all right. Just as we pulled into the hospital parking lot, the boy turned completely blue and I knew enough to yell: "He stopped breathing!" "We're here" was the only response I got. Hospital personnel grabbed the stretcher and wheeled the boy into the emergency room. Several police officers followed closely behind and after about 30 minutes it became evident that the boy was not going to survive. I saw tears coming down the cheeks of one Lansdale police officer and I guess I could only describe my mental state as pure shock.

Lieutenant Sarver (now deceased) and I picked up some supplies and drove back to the station house. I remember telling Wayne something to the effect of how rotten I felt that I could not do more. "Get over it kid, if you're gonna be any good at this, you gotta keep sh*t like that out of your mind" was the only advice I got. I spent the next two years seeing more and more human tragedy while training myself to turn a hard heart to the human tragedy of massive injuries, death and destruction I would roll up on hundreds of times as a corpsman for the VMSC. All this before I turned 18. As a former police officer I had numerous such encounters as well. Many of them have faded into past memories; some have not.

Years later, one such incident still occupies my memory. Arriving at the scene of an accident on Rt. 611 in Bucks County, Pennsylvania, I remember walking up to the side of a car that had just been hit head on by a pickup truck. In the passenger side of the car sat 18-year old Debra

Bader, a young college student who was getting a ride home with a friend. The right front tire of the pick up truck had blown and the impact caused the truck to hop up on the roof, smashing the windshield of the car and making the wheel of the truck strike the passenger (Debra) on the right side of her face. She was alive and breathing when I arrived. I remember grabbing her hand as she sobbed for her mom and saying something like –"Hang in there; the ambulance is on the way." She squeezed my hand and turned to look at me with her good eye, as the right side of her face had been completely destroyed. I don't know why I said it… perhaps it was because I had just converted to Christianity… but I said, "I'm going to pray for you." With that she stopped moaning, nodded her head up and down twice, and breathed her last. Nobody should die alone. Incidents like that stick with you, and have been a part of my life since I was 16 years old.

  I've probably performed CPR on victims more than 50 plus times in about thirty years. The last time I performed CPR since starting this book was at the Philadelphia Athletic club in Chalfont, Pennsylvania. Inside racquetball court #1 an acquaintance of mine, John Wilson, collapsed after playing a match with another friend of mine, John Walters. On that occasion all I heard was *THUD*. Turning around, I saw John Wilson lying on the racquetball floor in a most unnatural position. I rushed into the court, and flipped John over onto his back while his cousin Tim Wallace rushed to my side. After we realized John was not breathing, Tim began mouth to mouth resuscitation while I did chest compressions. This went on for several minutes while others watched and called 911. After what seemed like an eternity, I remember saying a silent prayer and saying to God 'if we only had a defibrillator.'

  At that instant, as I looked up, I saw a police officer heading for us, defibrillator in hand. I was thrilled that the

Lord had answered my prayer – or so I thought at the time – and I was equally confident we would be getting John back. My distance from the Lord grew even wider when John Wilson was later pronounced dead at the Doylestown hospital.

John and his wife were Christians – Baptists as I recall – and his death, like others I'll talk about later, were all part of God's plan to get me back in the family of God after running from Him for many years.

As a young man, I guess you could say I lived a charmed life. At 16, a rescue squad member, an ambulance attendant, and a police cadet. Co-Captain of my Junior High football team and later in senior high, named once honorary Co- Captain of the football team. That same year I was elected my high school class president.

Photo by Ted Aiken
For my first paying job, I was a
lifeguard at the local community pool.
July 4, 1976

At age 18, I served as a volunteer fireman and then became the youngest person to graduate from the Pennsylvania State Police Academy. Another young man, Mark Webster, and I were (to my knowledge) were the very first 18 year olds to graduate from that academy.

That's me as a police officer, 1977

Yes, I was 18 years old when I first became a police officer. You could not have told me then, but I realize now that I was too young. In fact, several years later they bumped the age back up to 21.

I think at a very early age I became addicted to two things. One was the attention I always seemed to receive, starting with my debut at age 15 as "Story-time Steve." This was a television production put on by some local librarians who superimposed me on Dr. Seuss books as I read and pointed out the pictures and words for young children. My series was seen by hundreds of public school children and I think I was hooked the first time a young boy pointed me out to his mother in a grocery store.

The other thing I became addicted to was adrenaline. I seemed to live for all the thrills I could glean from life and that was the toughest addiction of all to beat. When I was 21, as a police officer and volunteer fireman, I was in a gun battle in which the perpetrator was killed. This incident and one other in the 1980s led me to Christ. (more on that later)

After serving nine years as a police officer in the Philadelphia area, my career ended in the tiny little town of Trumbauersville, Pennsylvania. I could probably write an entire book just on my police experiences alone, but I'll spare you for another day. I continued what turned into an extremely successful 24-year bodyguard career, allowing me to work on a couple of presidential campaigns and meet two presidents. I also met two American vice presidents, a king or two, a former prime minister of Great Britain, several ambassadors, and senators and congressmen galore.

Guarding former British Prime Minister Margaret Thatcher

My distinguished bodyguard career led me to having breakfast with Beverly LaHaye, her husband Dr. Tim LaHaye, and Dr. Jerry Falwell the morning Bill Clinton was first elected president. It also allowed me to occasionally work security advances for Col. Oliver North, John Ashcroft, Billy Graham, Charles Stanley, Pat Buchanan, Margaret Thatcher, and many other famous and not-so-famous heroes. I did some security work for a band that became very famous – Daryl Hall & John Oates. Hall & Oates went on to record numerous gold and platinum albums. (Later, John's parents, Al and Ann, became good friends of mine with Mr. Oates (Al) even giving me my first racquetball lesson.)

One of the nicest bodyguard memories I have was staying in a holding room alone with Billy Graham before he spoke at a gathering of the National Religious Broadcasters. Rev. Graham struck up a 15 minute conversation with me as if he had known me all his life. At the time I was going through many personal struggles and he was the first person to point out to me that many of us look at our lives as if we were looking under a needlepoint creation – with strings hanging down and the appearance of disorder and chaos. Rev. Graham pointed out to me that God sees the top of the needlepoint. God sees the "big picture" and knows the beautiful side of our lives if we only put our trust in HIM. I've heard that analogy many times since, but THE Billy Graham told it to me in person.

For me the lesson is always really simple – do things God's way and get blessed, or do things my way and get benched, or worse.

The first lesson in recovery from traumatic experiences starts with your own, hard look and honest evaluation of yourself.

Examine yourselves to see whether you are in the faith; test yourselves. Do you not realize that Christ Jesus is in you—unless, of course, you fail the test? **2 Corinthians 13:5**

How important do you really think you are? Are you the type of person who may not say so but think the world revolves around you? In the Book of Job in the Old Testament, God asked Job some pretty poignant questions and made some statements.
Where were you when I... laid the foundations of the earth? What are those foundations attached to?
Or who shut in the sea with doors, when it burst forth and issued from the womb;...when I fixed My limit for it, and set bars and doors; when I said, This far you may come, but no farther, and here your proud waves must stop!
Shall the one who contends with the Almighty correct him? He who rebukes God, let him answer it."

By way of personal examples, I went from being the Grand Marshall of my hometown Christmas Parade to suffering a broken neck and ending up spending 74 days in jail for a crime I did not commit. With the help of the Lord, I was able to come back and become a lobbyist on Capitol Hill in Washington, D.C. and – later –host the fastest growing radio talk show in Arizona and run the campaign for a U.S. House of Representatives candidate. All this success – only to have everything come crashing down around me (again) in June of 2006. At that time I was given at least partial credit for removing a 22-year incumbent Congressman by the name of Jim Kolbe – a mission God may have given me back in 2001. More on that later. The point I'm getting ready to make is: I mess things up when I do things MY way, instead of God's!

On my very last radio show in Tucson, Arizona – right before the station manager pulled my show off the air

– I told the listening audience that, after going through everything, I have finally learned to judge my IMPORTANCE in life by an easy and simple method. This method is to first take a bucket of water and fill it so it overflows. Stick your arm in the bucket as far as you can, up to your elbow. Without spilling too much water, move your arm around, twist it, gently move it from side to side, and then slowly pull your arm out of the water. When your arm is fully removed, the hole that remains in the water is the measure of how important you are in this world. Now, to God you are so important it cannot be measured. But with the world, your importance is measured by that hole in the water.

Like you, I'm nothing more than a lump of clay. A lump of clay that had to be smashed a few times before things finally sank in. God elevated me – this piece of clay – to meet and learn from the "best" Christianity and society had to offer – only to have the "clay" think he knew better, causing the "potter" to smash him and start all over. Losing my house, our mission for homeless teenagers, and almost losing my family; then after "recovering," almost twelve years later, it happened all over again – only this time, book in hand, I was REALLY ok with what happened to me.

"ONWARD CHRISTIAN SOLDIER"

The next words are "Fighting as to war." The Apostle Paul who wrote nearly three quarters of the New Testament said: "fight the good fight," "press on," "finish the race."

Regardless of how you might picture the "struggle" to be "Christ-like," **BEING CHRIST-LIKE IS WHAT CHRISTIANS ARE CALLED TO BE!**

There are no exceptions. It's that simple – when you're in the family, (the Army of God if you will), it is demanded of the commander in chief that you "be conformed to his image!" I'm convinced the battle to be conformed to His image is a battle against SELF – a battle of constantly choosing between our own self-indulgences, self-esteem, and self-gratification versus those of a Creator God who requires us to shed "self" and replace it with *Christ-likeness*. I don't think the battle ends until we draw our last breath. For some, "self" becomes their only god. It is a false god for sure but one that far too many serve all the days of their lives!

      These teachings are seldom heard from pulpits today, primarily because society, with the help of the liberal media, has lynched so many Christians. Locally and on television, Christians have been made to look like buffoons, Jim Jones-like, or David Koresh-like by twisting the intent of the Word of God and marginalizing Christians at every turn. Let me give you an example.

      Probably no one in recent history that I am aware of has been called more names for what he believes than Jerry Falwell. Unfortunately, while this book was being printed, Rev. Falwell went home to be with the Lord in May of 2007. Misquoted and taken out of context, Rev. Falwell saw it all. Jerry Falwell was certainly not without a mistake or two – after all he was only human. I met Reverend Falwell on many occasions and on at least one, he shocked me by remembering my first name! I later learned he's one of those guys who had a knack for remembering names. I deeply respected Reverend Falwell, but whether you agreed or disagreed with his theology, he was man who took Jesus with him everywhere he went. It could have been face to face television debates or interviews, Jerry Falwell stood up for what he believed and I love that! I'm an in your face kind of guy – I was always acting that way in the town where I grew up. There have been many controversial reports written by me and about me in my local paper. But unlike Reverend Falwell, I had to learn the importance of I Corinthians 13. If you don't know what I'm talking about, please take the time to dust off a Bible and follow me.

The late, Dr. Jerry Falwell

Many "Christians" today cringe at the thought of the community they serve thinking of them as some sort of "nut-job" – or that they are "fanatics" and not of the "mainstream." Their reputations become their most prized possession. This is why, year after year, we see more members of the clergy buckling under the pressure to steer clear of controversial subjects like the detrimental effects of homosexuality on society today or abortion. Those promoting the radical, homosexual agenda will not stop until they have silenced us regarding this subject. Silencing the pulpits is just a few short years away – we need only look to the countries of Canada, France, and Sweden for the blueprint of what will eventually take place in the United States.

Barring a miracle from God Himself, soon it will be against the law or a "hate crime" to speak out against the abhorrent behavior and perversion that is part and parcel of the radical homosexual movement. It's already starting to happen in various pockets around the world and here in the United States. In January of 2005, Illinois Governor Rod

Blagojevich signed into law "hate crimes" legislation. This was the first time in the country a law of this type, did not exempt religious organizations. As of this writing, under the new law, any Jewish organization can be forced, under this new "progressive" law to hire Muslims.

In 2007, Senate bill 2 in Oregon was another glaring example. If passed, it would limit free speech in Christian churches about homosexuality and require teaching in public schools that homosexuality is an accepted lifestyle. Nick Graham of the Oregon Family Council said, "This is possibly the most dangerous piece of legislation to come from Oregon's legislature." It won't be very long before Congress tries to enact similar legislation at the federal level. We are losing this portion of the culture war. I wonder how long Almighty God will allow the San Francisco court house to stand before He levels it as "another" warning to us all, but will we listen? The same political correctness prevents many today from speaking out against radical Muslims.

As you'll read later, there is not a horrible name under the sun that I have not been called in one form or another.

Take the case of Jimmy Swaggart. People are quick to dismiss him as a "has been" or a "loser," or much worse, because with his failings, he proved himself to be a fallible human being. Who among us isn't fallible? The Bible tells us that "all have sinned and come short of the Glory of God." **Romans 3:23**. All, not some.

The Bible goes on to say in I John 1:8 and 9 that: "If we say we have no sin, we deceive ourselves, and the truth is not in us. (Yet,) if we confess our sins, he is faithful and just to forgive us of our sins, and to cleanse us from all unrighteousness."

The word "confess" there literally means to "agree." If we agree with God that we have sinned against Him, this cleanses us from the filth and the dirt that so besets all of us. WHAT A DEAL!

Come now, and let us reason together, says the Lord: though your sins be as scarlet, they shall be as white as snow; though they be red like crimson, they shall be as wool. **Isaiah 1:18**

Many have discounted Swaggart's ability to teach. This is crucially wrong and flies in the face of Galatians 6: 1and 2. I'm not talking about a so called "man of God" who continues to sin on and on and never becomes accountable to anyone. That type is the real hypocrite, the Peter Popoff's of the world. (You may have seen the movie "Leap of Faith," starring Steve Martin. Peter Popoff is the preacher who in real life got caught using a secret microphone and a receiver in his ear to claim hearing from God. In reality it is only his wife behind the curtain giving him tips that they previously gleaned from the audience to make their act convincing! Popoff continues to peddle his snake-oil, 'get rich' schemes in the name of the Lord.)

No, I'm talking about "real men" who make mistakes. At what point do we say this man is a piece of garbage, he can never be used again? The answer is – we don't! Yes we judge the fruits, but never the person. We are all garbage according to the Bible. **Romans 3:10**

The ONLY thing that makes us clean is accepting personally what Jesus did for us on the cross. So who are we to judge Jimmy Swaggart or anybody else? It is my contention that the Assembly of God (the denomination that held Jimmy Swaggart's pastoral credentials before it defrocked him) – and Christianity in general for that matter

– is either not equipped or is unwilling to help the Jimmy Swaggart's (their own former leaders) back toward a place of service to God. Yes, the Christian army is the only army in the world that shoots its own wounded and this should not be the case!

While living in Washington, D.C., I saw Jimmy Swaggart preach on TV. It was September $23^{rd\ 2001}$, exactly 12 days after the September 11th Pentagon and WTC bombings. Rev. Swaggart spoke (I believe) prophetically about the Muslim religion.

Me & Jimmy Swaggart (late 80's)

I'm familiar enough with Jimmy Swaggart Ministries to know the show was taped months in advance. What he said is not important right now – my point is this: if Rev. Swaggart, or anybody else for that matter, is truly is an instrument of God, who are we to discount everything he says?

Jerry Falwell – who, to my knowledge, had never had a moral failure – speaks words of truth and the media twisted his words and take him out of context. Jimmy Swaggart speaks words of truth but nobody (relatively speaking) will listen to him anymore!

I still watch Jimmy on TV whenever I get the chance; he's my brother in the Lord. In general, however, people would rather focus on the messenger instead of on the message. In their minds, it gives them license to ignore! I was the same way. I found myself judging the messenger(s) and using my "judgment" of them as the sole basis as to whether I was going to accept their advise or not. Bad, bad idea. This is why the Bible works so hard teaching Christians NOT to be judgmental. In doing so, we cut ourselves off from a lot of the blessings and a lot of "healing".

> *Judge Not, that you be not judged.*
> **Matt 7:1**

These days, the United States military, stretched as thin as it is, must coordinate all attacks. The Air Force must coordinate with the Navy, the Navy with the Marines, and so on. No greater example of this took place than in the war in Iraq to oust Saddam Hussein. I'm told our military moved more troops and equipment further and faster than any army in the history of the world! Born-again believers are way overdue to begin fighting the "good fight" mentioned in 1 Timothy 6:12 – together! That has been the problem all along for the Jerry Falwells of the world and other men of God. The press and the liberals can't get him in the sexual arena; they can't get him on finances. It's not just Jerry Falwell, there are millions of Christians as well as preachers in this country. Many are on TV and radio as well and they "get it." So when they can't debate you

38

intellectually they resort to calling you names or trying to dig up dirt to discredit people. This holds true for the thousands of preachers and church leaders nationwide that never go public beyond their own church walls.

Here's my point. The problem we are faced with – all people of faith and those like us who are 'Born Again' – is that we have common ground. We are right, as in correct. It would be easy for us to get our "religion" out of people's faces. I mean how much easier could your life be if you did not have to be so concerned with trying to spread the Gospel? What a horrible thing God does to us by suggesting we tell people how to be happy and live forever in Heaven. After all, we have to get the kids off to school. There are dentist appointments, after school activities, problems with the mortgage, the car, hassles, you name it. It's a wonder any of us makes it to church more than twice a year! Oh how the world has diluted us!

Those who die lost without having received Christ's grace, making Him their personal Savior, are doomed. We are OBLIGATED to try to warn them. Certainly, though portrayed otherwise it is a massage of love not hate, of hope, not despair. If our message were not true, why would the world be trying so hard to shut us up? As much as we tell them it is not a matter of religion and that it IS actually a matter of a relationship with an actual person we know to be alive – most will still not listen. A few will, and that is all we are responsible for. We are never held accountable for the results, just the efforts. With all due respect to our Muslim "friends," Mohammed is dead. Just like every other person on the face of the earth, except for Jesus Christ. Buddha is dead; Joseph Smith is dead; Joseph Stalin is dead; Emperor Hirohito is dead. None of us is getting out of here alive. Our sentence from God since the fall of man has been a sentence of DEATH. There is only one way to get a stay of execution in life and it's NOT through any man or philosophy. It is, however, found in Christ.

Chapter 2
THE OTHER DATE THAT WILL LIVE IN INFAMY

There are certainly more dramatic and heart-wrenching stories about 9-11 than those of my family and I. In no way do I wish to compare our experiences with those who lost loved ones on that dreadful day, so I will gloss over many of the details in order to make my "God-point."

As almost everyone who reads this will remember, September 11, 2001, started out like any other day. I was working as the Director of Communications for the Traditional Values Coalition (TVC), living at 139 C St. S.E., just 932 feet from the property of our nation's capitol. That morning, I was working on a press release for a piece of legislation. At 8:46 a.m. American Airlines Flight 11 hit the North Twin Tower in New York. At about 8:50 a.m. I received a call from Phil Sheldon (son of TVC founder Rev. Lou Sheldon) who said – "I guess we won't be putting out a press release today." When I asked him why, he said, "Turn on your TV – a plane just crashed into the World Trade Center." I hung up the phone and told both Rev. Sheldon and his daughter Andria to turn on the TV. As we watched the smoking tower on the tube I remember making the comment: "I'll bet it's terrorists." Rev Lou looked at me in half disbelief and half disgust and said, "NO! Do you think that's possible?" At 9:02 a.m. United Flight 175 crashed into the South Twin Tower. I honestly do not remember whether we actually got to see the second tower being crashed into live or footage of it happening just seconds later. Either way, the results were the same – pure shock! I looked out the window of our second story offices at TVC to see a plethora of military trucks, Secret Service type vehicles, police cars racing up and down the streets – already D.C. looked like chaos.

My wife Deborah's daily routine was to take our daughter Sarah to the Christian school where Sarah was a senior. Sarah's school was not far from the southwest side of Pentagon building – directly opposite from where we lived. I called Deborah on her cell phone and told her, "I think we are going to war." She asked me what I meant and we both decided that it would be best for her to get Sarah and bring her home for the day.

Directly across the street from where I lived and worked is the back of the Madison Building.

The Madison Building in Washington

Federal officers guard the delivery entrance there and over the weeks, I became friendly with most of the fellows who worked that thankless post. My closest guess is that it was about 9:20 a.m. when I asked the guard on duty if he had heard anything else with regards to this "attack" and he told me another plane was headed towards D.C. and that the city was being evacuated.

At about 9:38 a.m. that fateful morning, my daughter Stephanie and I felt the rush of a sonic boom go through us as we heard the terrible explosion of Flight 77 crashing into the Pentagon. We had no idea where or what the explosion was but I remember thinking to myself that we were being attacked and at war. I later learned that Barbara Olsen – whom I had met on at least one occasion – was on that flight. Immediately it seemed all communications were cut off in the city. I later found out that in the event of a national crisis, the military essentially secures all cell and land line phones just in case it needs them. After learning that the plane many had heard so low to the ground just a few minutes before, actually crashed in or near the Pentagon, I realized that my wife and daughter had to have been very close when it hit. I knew almost to the minute how long it took Deborah to drive back from the school. I correctly deduced that they would have been on Rt. 395 that wraps around the east side of the Pentagon, very close to the building. In that one short instance of not knowing what was fact or what was rumor, it occurred to me that by telling Deborah to pick up Sarah and come home, I may in fact have killed my own wife and daughter. I started to lose it. By now congressional staffers were pouring out of the Cannon Congressional Building, ghostly white faces on the men and mascara running down the eyes of women – many crying silently or in hysterics. I saw one woman drop to her knees right on the curb and stretch out her hands to the sky while screaming: "Oh God save us!"

Rev. Sheldon and I prayed with some people on C St. who were wandering about in total shock. At that point I told Rev. Lou that I wanted to get my daughter Stephanie out of the city because we all knew another plane was coming. I felt like a coward for leaving but I knew that

Stephanie's safety had to come first: I am her father! Rev. Lou said only two words to me – "yes, go." Stephanie and I prayed, and then quickly packed a backpack with water, a couple of apples, a flashlight, a pocket-knife and my handgun. Little did I know then that the whole time I lived in D.C. I was apparently in violation of local city ordinances prohibiting the keeping of guns in your own house! (Fortunately, in June of 2008, the U.S. Supreme court overturned that ridicules infringement of our second Amendment rights.) Deborah had our only car so Stephanie and I gassed up a little two stroke motorized skateboard I owned and we headed out of the city towards the Pentagon to find my wife and Sarah. On this little scooter that barely held me alone, Stephanie and I weaved in and out of the log jammed traffic. Crossing over the foot bridge that connects D.C. with the Pentagon we actually made pretty good time as we headed towards that majestic five-sided building with smoke billowing out of it. Stephanie and I stopped to help everyone we could, whether it was a disabled motorist or a person so distraught she was paralyzed with fear. Still no word from Deborah or Sarah, we pressed on to the location where I thought they were when the plane hit.

The actual scooter!

Not finding our car anywhere on Rt. 395, we headed southwest to the other side of the Pentagon and towards Sarah's school where I hoped they had retreated for safety. Stephanie and I rode, walked, and carried that little scooter through woods, through a small village, and eventually to the home of Andrea Sheldon Lafferty where both Sarah and Deborah were waiting – safe and sound.

Deborah and Sarah were southeast of the Pentagon when it was hit and did get engulfed by the ensuing smoke. They managed to pull over and eventually were told by a police officer that they could not go back into D.C. and that they would have to turn around. Around 11:00 a.m. they worked their way to the Lafferty house; Stephanie and I arrived about six hours later. When the plane hit the Pentagon all Deborah and Sarah saw and heard was what they imagined was a bomb being dropped on D.C. Because I originally told Deborah "I think we are going to war" she had no idea about any planes hitting any buildings. When we finally met each other tears of joy flowed freely as we thought they were dead and they thought we were dead. You COULD say we were the GRATEFUL DEAD!

At 10:26 a.m. American Flight 93 crashed in a field in Pennsylvania. We later learned that men like **Todd Beamer** and **Jeremy Glick** and other passengers, in the purest American tradition, tried to subdue the cowardly hijackers who evidently buried the plane nose first into the ground rather than surrender to the "infidels." Figuratively speaking, these brave American heroes may have saved our lives. They certainly saved many, many lives on that dreadful day.

Let's Roll!

Todd Beamer

Jeremy Glick

Although immediate conventional wisdom from the media was that Flight 93 was probably heading to crash the White House, I knew the target was the dome of the Capitol Building and stated so back then. The 9-11 Commission later confirmed my theory. I based my suspicion on several factors – not the least of which was that the dome was a more obvious and easier target. Many years prior to 9-11, I was on a private charter plane with Beverly LaHaye and our pilot actually received permission to fly over the White House lawn, something that today is inconceivable. Even back then I realized how difficult it was to spot the White House from the air. Had Flight 93 coming from the northwest crashed into the dome of the Capitol, it surely would have spread debris all over the southeast side – the side we were living on. The plane very easily could have taken out the Madison Building and ended up literally in our front yard. We talk about losing 3000 of our fellow American citizens that day. I'm afraid when all of the rescue workers and 9-11 volunteers succumb to their respective respiratory and other 9-11 related illnesses, the death toll may well climb.

Me at the Pentagon September 14, 2001

NOT LONG AFTER 9-11

Soon after that fateful September day, the great anthrax scare started in D.C. Several postal workers in the D.C. area contracted anthrax – among them was the delivery carrier for our house. Another postal worker was killed from complications resulting from inhaling anthrax spores. Washington was essentially under siege at that time. Years later, Dr. Steven Hatfill was held out as a "person of interest," but the U.S. Attorney General
eventually was forced to admit he was wrong and that Dr. Hatfill had nothing to do with it. In June of 2008, Dr.

Hatfill was awarded almost 6 million dollars in punitive damages.

Deborah and another girl who worked at the TVC had to take Cypro capsules; these made Deborah very sick. By this time anyone in D.C. who received a mosquito or an insect bite of any kind or who had a chest cold or influenza of any kind would visit the doctor. No doctors I am aware of were taking any chances and Cypro was handed out like candy. The Cypro Deborah took made her stomach so sick, it was then she (jokingly) said she was leaving Washington with or without me! By Christmas 2001 we left the Traditional Values Coalition and Washington, D.C. (More on that later)

Sometime in November of 2001, while still living in Washington, I was a guest on "The Sheila Jackson Show" on KPAM radio in Oregon. I was speaking about the "end of the world" after September 11. As a matter of fact, that particular radio show and topic led us to use "It's the end of the world as we know it" by REM as our theme music for "Straight from the Hip," my former radio show. We used it right up until the end. One of the topics I brought up is that people don't like to think about the end of the world anymore than they like to think about their own mortality. It is a theme I have carried with me for many years.

And so, our task is to show the world we know the answers without looking like "jerks," "bigots," "know-it-alls," "pompous," "greedy," "ignorant," "narcissistic," or any other human quality that can be attributed to the negative side of life. Once you get that down, you have it made. Get over yourself, it's NEVER GOING TO HAPPEN! No matter how close you come to "living a pure life," when you proclaim the Gospel of Jesus Christ you will get attacked. How many "divisions" will come to your rescue? You'll be "lucky" if you get a care package from the Red Cross. You will be attacked, at least verbally. That does not mean we have been absolved of our DUTY.

The world spends an inordinate amount of time trying to paint "Christians" in a negative light. Comedians like Bill Maher see people of "faith" as nothing more than cannon fodder for verbal assaults of any variety. The idea of disrespecting and insulting Christians or Conservatives is sport to them. They rarely, if ever, allow themselves to be placed in a position where they have to answer for their own inane philosophies of life. Instead, people like Maher choose to take long distance pot-shots for the cheap laughs and are never held accountable or put themselves in a position to be challenged.

I'm "old-school", but I still believe that "God and Country" are not curse words! From the time I was a high school football player to today, I still get teary eyed when I hear the Star Spangled Banner and I still remove my hat. I still respect the American flag enough not let it touch the ground. Like many of you, I actually believe what I say when I pledge allegiance to the flag! I still believe that the United States of America is the greatest country on the face of the earth and I still believe some things are worth dying for! I am naïve enough to respect those who left their families, lost their lands, and gave up their lives so that we can be free, and that they deserve to be held in respect and in reverence.

Dumbing down children

Yes, thanks to the likes of Madelyn Murray O'Hair, Michael Newdow, the ACLU and all the ilk of the "progressive left," we are now seeing an entire generation that was raised with the idea that everything that made this country great, everything "good" about this country, is to be held in sheer disdain, to be discarded or eliminated at any and every opportunity!

* Dear God:
Why didn't you save the school children at
Moses Lake , Washington 2/2/96
Bethel , Alaska 2/19/97
Pearl , Mississippi 10/1/97
West Paducah , Kentucky 12/1/97
Stamp, Arkansas 12/15/97
Jonesboro , Arkansas 3/24/98
Edinboro , Pennsylvania 4/24/98
Fayetteville , Tennessee 5/19/98
Springfield , Oregon 5/21/98
Richmond , Virginia 6/15/98
Littleton , Colorado 4/20/99
Taber , Alberta , Canada 5/28/99
Conyers , Georgia 5/20/99
Deming , New Mexico 11/19/99
Fort Gibson , Oklahoma 12/6/99
Santee , California 3/ 5/01
El Cajon , California 3/22/01 and
Blacksburg, Virginia 4/16/07
Sincerely,
A Concerned Student

Dear Concerned Student:
I am not allowed in school anymore.
Sincerely,
God

How did this get started? Let's see, It started when Madeline Murray O'Hare complained she didn't want any prayer in our schools. We said, OK. Then, someone said you better not read the Bible in School, the Bible that says "thou shalt not kill, thou shalt not steal, and love your neighbors as yourself," and we said, OK. Dr. Benjamin Spock said we shouldn't spank our children when they misbehaved because their little personalities would be warped and we might damage their self-esteem. And we said, an expert should know what he's talking about so we said OK and won't spank them anymore. Then someone said teachers and principals better not discipline our children when they misbehave and we said OK. And the school administrators said no faculty member in this school better touch a student when they misbehave because we don't want any bad publicity, and we surely don't want to be sued. And we said OK. Then someone said, let's let our daughters have abortions if they want, and they won't even have to tell their parents. And we said OK, that's a great idea. Then some wise school board member said, since boys will be boys and they're going to do it anyway, let's give our sons all the condoms they want, so they can have all the fun they desire, and we won't have to tell their parents they got them at school. And we said OK, that's another great idea. Then some of our top elected officials said it doesn't matter what we do in private as long as we do our jobs. And we said, it doesn't matter what anybody, including the President, does in private as long as we have jobs and the economy is good. And someone else took that appreciation a step further and published pictures of nude children and then stepped further still by making them available on the Internet. And we said OK, everyone's entitled to free speech. And the entertainment industry said, let's make TV shows and movies that promote profanity, violence and illicit sex. And let's record music that encourages rape, drugs, murder, suicide, and satanic themes. And we said OK, it's just entertainment and it has no adverse effect and nobody takes it seriously anyway, so go right ahead. Now we're asking ourselves why our children have no conscience, why they don't know right

51

from wrong, and why it doesn't bother them to kill strangers, classmates or even themselves. Undoubtedly, if we thought about it long and hard enough, we could figure it out. I'm sure it has a great deal to do with..."WE REAP WHAT WE SOW," *AUTHOR UNKNOWN*

Feel free to pray for people like Bill Maher if you care to, (after all if there is breath, there is hope). However, don't ever think that as a man or woman of God any of us needs to kowtow to the likes of him or anyone else in that vein. There will always be evil people in the world, people who constantly try to tear down all that is good about this Country! With world events being what they are today, none of us knows how much time anyone has left. Don't be afraid to shake the *dust off your feet*. **Acts 13:51.** As for the "Bill Mahers" of this world, there are plenty more out there who actually will listen to you! It's not necessary to be "fanatical" to the point that your message is muted completely. Take for instances the "Christian man" who, on November 9, 2001, interrupted President George W. Bush before a speech on the war against terrorism. The unidentified man chided the President for not discussing (in his mind) the "real issues of importance," biblical principals. Or the man who interrupted Presidential Candidate Mitt Romney in February of 2007, rebuking him because he (Romney) is not a "Christian." The world and the main stream media does enough to make us look foolish and out of touch, we don't need the actions of self-proclaimed, self righteous, false prophet fools, painting a bleaker picture of the "Christian-life." than is already widely accepted. Remember – **you do not have to commit intellectual suicide to be a Christian.** I'm sorry, but President Bush was elected to be our Commander in chief not preacher in chief. The popularity of my radio show about religion and politics did not qualify me to be a pastor. I was, a news commentator who has a similar faith in Jesus

Christ. That's it. I'm sorry to disappoint those who think I did not do enough to "evangelize."

On the road to recovery I suppose, as I step further and further out in faith, I know to expect more and more attacks on my character personally. This was brought to the forefront when I was released as campaign manager in Arizona's Eighth Congressional District after taking on a congressional bully by the name of Jim Kolbe. At the time, Kolbe was known as 'Cardinal' and it was my fiercest political battle to take him on and help force him into an early retirement. (More on that later.) Before I even finished this book, liberal blogs had already started in on me. My past will no doubt make me seem vulnerable, as certain elements in society will stop at nothing to discredit me, marginalize me, and demonize me. Saint Paul called it a "Thorn in the Flesh," but God bless them too!!!

I am concerned about the current ecumenical drive among mainstream denominations that seems to be accompanying our current renewed patriotism after September 11, 2001. Yes, we are all Americans; yes, we share the common virtue of freedom. U.S. history is replete with people who have gladly laid down their lives to protect our most cherished asset – freedom – but when it comes to religion(s) there can be no compromise. We cannot expect Muslims to compromise their core beliefs against homosexuality, the position of women in society, and other things the Koran teaches or is alleged to teach. Nor should we expect fundamental Christians to compromise our core beliefs that – apart from salvation through Christ – no person can expect eternal life in heaven. Given the opportunity, would I stand arm in arm with a person whose religious views are different from mine to attain a specific goal? Sure I would. But that does not mean either one of us agrees with the other about our fundamental religious beliefs.

Make no mistake about it, the way I read my Bible tells me the Muslim religion is damning millions of people to an eternity in hell without God. Contrary to what the liberal media would have you believe, the Koran is replete with calls of violence against Christians, Jews, "infidels," and non-believers. For a very long time the following, marked by (*), was on my Web site, *author unknown*.
*Can a devout Muslim be an American patriot and a loyal citizen? Consider this:

Theologically, no – because his allegiance is to Allah, the moon god of Arabia.

Religiously, no – because no other religion is accepted by his Allah except Islam. **Quran 2:256**

Socially, no – because his allegiance to Islam forbids him to make friends with Christians or Jews.

Scripturally, no. Because his allegiance is to the five pillars of Islam and the Quran (Koran).

54

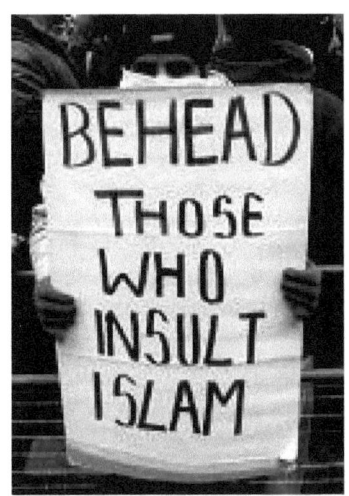

Domestically, no – because he is instructed to beat and scourge his wife when she disobeys him. **Quran 4:34**

Politically, no – because he must submit to the mullahs (spiritual leaders), who teach annihilation of Israel and destruction of America, the great Satan.

Intellectually, no – because he cannot accept the American Constitution since it is based on Biblical principles and he believes the Bible to be corrupt.

Geographically, no – because his allegiance is to Mecca, to which he turns in prayer five times a day.

Philosophically, no – because Islam, Muhammad, and the Quran do not allow freedom of religion and expression.

Democracy and Islam cannot co-exist.

Spiritually, no – because when we declare "one nation under God," the Christian God is loving and kind while Allah is NEVER referred to as our heavenly father, nor is he ever called love in the Quran's 99 excellent names.

....perhaps we should be very suspicious of ALL MUSLIMS in this country. They obviously cannot be both good Muslims and good Americans. Call it what you wish...it's still the truth. The more who understand this, the better it will be for our country. *Author unknown *end*

Something is very wrong in this country when a Muslim can enter a Jewish school in Seattle, shoot six women and kill one, and the police and the media become more concerned with protecting local area mosques and Muslims than protecting the rest of us. Something is very wrong in this country when our own politicians try to convey "rights" to Terrorists while hanging our own American Soldiers or intelligence Officers out to dry. What's wrong with this picture?

To avoid looking foolish, Christian pastors and leaders in many churches have begun to acquiesce to the world's demand for "tolerance" in order to appeal to the broader masses and the message of uniformity to be CHRIST-LIKE is already beginning to dim. I have no problem tolerating views that are different from mine. But to remain silent or to allow our opinions as Christians to be silenced or labeled as "hate speech," is pure hypocrisy on the part of those who preach tolerance for all views, except ours. The U.S. Constitution guarantees us FREEDOM OF SPEECH; this must include ALL speech, even if it is considered "offensive!" Watered down Gospel messages only feed half as many sheep! Do they do ANY good? I'm sure they do, after all God can use a jackass if He wants to. Ten years ago I would have judged those politically correct pastors and been just as critical as many are of me today. But that's ok, my "thorn in the flesh" keeps me humble and I am grateful for it.

Getting back to my point: I can't tell you how many good preachers, good men of God I've seen absolutely dissipate when they get on radio or TV. Having been knowledgeable of and friends with workers in some of the largest evangelical national ministries, I HAVE SEEN MY FAIR SHARE OF people who could have done so much more for the Lord, but they crumbled when faced with the most disarming question any reporter can ask a "Born Again believer." **DO YOU REALLY BELIEVE THAT?**

As Christians, we have NEVER been called to "compromise" in this regard. After all, a "compromise" is nothing more than a partial surrender. So when asked, **do you really believe that,** what is the answer? The answer is for men and women of God to, collectively and individually, start speaking up. As I said earlier, **SAY WHAT YOU MEAN AND MEAN WHAT YOU SAY!**

For those Christians who are paying attention, I'm not telling you anything new when I say that this country is headed to hell in a hand-basket! When Christian television networks refuse to air programs with men like Hal Lindsey, or these same networks are allowed to placate the radical lobbyists, we are in deep trouble! Such was the case not too long ago when Mr. Lindsey left the Trinity Broadcasting Network for what he considered to be efforts to muzzle his opinions about radical Islam. *Later on Mr. Lindsey returned.*

For some reason, as a part-time bodyguard for 24 years I became close to a lot of influential people. Whether I was on a treadmill with Pat Buchanan or driving cross-country with Beverly LaHaye. I learned the "greats" have one thing in common – apart from their belief in the God of the Bible – it is their unwavering ability to stand up and be counted for what they believe, no matter the cost. Rubbing elbows with many of the nation's most influential Christian and political leaders, there was a time when I was brazen enough to think God was calling me somehow to "minister" to these famous people. A good example of that was my work with Pat Buchanan. Although my one on one conversations with Mr. Buchanan were limited, I came to realize that he, like others I met over the years, had forgotten more about world history than I'll ever know.

Pat Buchanan and my family in 1996
I traveled extensively with Pat Buchanan – this photo was taken one day when I had a layover in Philly and my family came to say hello to Dad.

The only area I felt I was up to par with Pat Buchanan was the Bible. However, God wasn't necessarily calling me to 'minister' to the likes of Pat Buchanan. HE WAS CALLING ME TO BE MORE LIKE Him, yes – CHRIST-LIKE! Pat Buchanan Christ-like? Yes – with a resolute faith in God and unwavering stance to stand up for what he believes, this, in my opinion, is a "Christ-like" quality.

Trust me when I tell you, most of these "big shots" I met or worked for or worked with, are big shots because they truly believe they are doing the right thing for God and Country. From what I have observed first-hand behind the scenes, most of them are really, truly, doing good things. Certainly, I met those whose motives are highly suspect. Of all the national ministries I either worked for or know of, I only have knowledge of one that is a bogus organization, although I'm sure there are others Even the "greats" are not perfect! Far from it – neither am I; neither are you. Learn from them! Just about everybody I know enjoys meeting famous people – it's a bit of a thrill and the Lord allowed me to walk down that path for many years. Not only did I meet many of the "greats," I had the opportunity to spend a lot of time with some of them, gleaning an education one cannot get in any school in the country.

In the Shadow of Phyllis Schlafly

Beverly LaHaye, founder of Concerned Women for America, www.CWFA.org was a client with whom I spent a great deal of time. I traveled with Mrs. LaHaye on numerous occasions and ran security for her national conventions 20-plus years in a row. Over the years we had a few scary moments, mostly encountering militant homosexuals who would throw objects at us or just generally try to disrupt meetings where Mrs. LaHaye spoke. It started way back in the early 1980s at a hotel in Crystal City, Virginia, when a false fire alarm was pulled by a group of radical homosexuals from "ACT-UP." Without divulging any "family secrets", I can assure you that if any "outsider" ever had the opportunity to see hypocrisy with Tim and Bev LaHaye that person is me. There simply was none to be found. Of course, they are human just like you and me, but two finer Christian leaders are nowhere to be found in my lifetime. I may not agree with everything they say or teach but that is of no consequence. I was more than willing to lay down my life in protection of theirs – it was my honor to keep them safe while they ministered to thousands. On numerous occasions, I met Phyllis Schlafly as well. Although Mrs. Schlafly would not know me if she passed me on the street, she has been a guest on my radio show several times. Phyllis Schlafly has been credited with almost single-handedly defeating the ERA (Equal Rights Amendment), a credit she rightly deserves. However, the unsung hero of defeating the ERA is Beverly LaHaye and the gallant members of Concerned Women for America. Although she received a fraction of the accolades Phyllis Schlafly got, in my opinion, Beverly LaHaye truly has never gotten the recognition she deserved for steering our country clear of the misnamed bill and detrimental effects of the ERA.

The Equal Rights Amendment…..sounds good doesn't it? EQUAL rights for women – who could possibly be against that? I'm not opposed to equal pay for women doing the same job as their male counterparts; nor would I ever want to see women denied anything their hearts desire in this great country of ours. After all, I raised three women and I have been married to the same one for over 26 years now.
NO, on the practical side, the Equal Rights Amendment was nothing more than a smoke screen concocted by the Left to increase and perhaps double the amount of payroll taxes withheld, and to help expedite the bullet train towards socialism in this country. For those in the know, it was hardly about ideology; it was always about the money! On the spiritual side, the ERA is a tool of dark forces to weaken the God given foundation of the nuclear family!

The fact that a nuclear family – one mom, one dad – has historically been THE best method of raising children could be damned. By splintering the traditions of family and marriage through the ERA and later with the radical homosexual agenda, those on the Left who prefer a socialist or globalist approach to government can be assured of victory in the coming years. This is why we see such a rise in power of radical homosexuality. With the help of the ACLU and others, they continue to attack and dictate everything from the Ten Commandments to what our children are taught in public schools. As long as we allow the FOUNDATIONS of this great country to continue to be marginalized and crumble, they will win.

I remember guarding Mrs. LaHaye once at a hotel in Crystal City when a group of radical homosexuals were protesting her presence. They were actually carrying picket signs with Phyllis Schafly's photo on it instead of Mrs. LaHaye's – no respect or no awareness. Mrs. LaHaye later went on to be an honorary member of the Board of Directors of the YouthQuest mission my wife Deborah and I ran near Philadelphia. As you can see, I cannot say enough good things about her or her husband – or her entire family for that matter.

Beverly LaHaye

Looking back over the years I can see that all of my "success" led me to terribly miscalculate my own abilities. In other words, my head was swelling with pride as I began to think of myself as invincible and began leaving behind the God I was supposed to be serving.

Chapter 3
BEFORE A FALL, ALWAYS PRIDE!

While I was a police officer, two incidents literally led me to Christ: the gun battle I will describe below and another incident in which I should have been killed.

The first situation in 1979 that led me to a realization about God involved a gun battle. At the time, William Livezey was one of the biggest methamphetamine dealers in Pennsylvania. He had his own brother killed for the life insurance money and had sworn he would not be taken alive. After lobbing tear gas into the house where Livezey had barricaded himself, the tear gas canisters set the house on fire. (Actual photo above) As the blaze grew, Sgt. Bruce Hemmerle, another volunteer fireman who was also a police officer, and I were selected to enter the house wearing our guns, a Scott air-pack and carrying a two and half inch fire hose. As we entered the second story of the house, now engulfed in flames, we heard the POP of one last shot as Livesey ended his own life. I accidentally ended up crawling over Livezey's dead body at the top of the stairs, unable to see him lying there because of the thick smoke.

That night, after about 30 hours of adrenaline induced sleeplessness, I finally started to drift off asleep. I was at that stage where you are half-asleep and half awake when I heard an audible voice (it sounded like mine) say, **"What would have happened if it were you lying there dead instead of him?"** I literally bolted up in bed, wondering how this voice could have sounded so real. I then began to ponder the actual question. With seven years of Catholic school to my name and a deceased, Bible-believing, grandmother, I did not have an answer! I did not want to believe that when we die, we simply drift off into the nothingness of some great abyss. To this day one of my favorite verses in the Bible is Jeremiah, Chapter 29, Verse 13, where God said: *And you shall seek me, and find me, when you shall search for me with all your heart.*

I started searching, and it took me three years to finally stumble across the plan of Salvation and to learn it is a gift from God known as GRACE. It cannot be earned and is not found in any man-made religions.

Do you really believe that? Yes, yes I do.

The second incident that got my attention was not nearly as dramatic but certainly had the potential to be just as deadly. I received a call from a pharmacy on Rt. 309 (a major highway that connects Philadelphia with Allentown, Pennsylvania, and is also used for a great deal of drug running). The pharmacist had caught a man trying to pass a forged prescription. When I pulled up to the pharmacy, the pharmacist pointed to a white vehicle pulling away with one male driver. Alone in my patrol car, I caught up to the suspect vehicle, activating my red and blue lights while the suspect driver pulled over to the side of the road. To this day, I do not know why I did not approach the vehicle to ask the driver for identification as I had done hundreds of times before. Maybe it was because I was not wearing my bulletproof vest on this hot August afternoon. Maybe there really are guardian angels who watch over us in these kinds of circumstances? Whatever the reason, I instructed the driver to exit the vehicle and walk towards me at the back of his car. Today they call these "felony stops." By then the pharmacist had arrived and pointed out the driver I was detaining as the man who tried to fill the bogus prescription for Dilauded. A minute or two later, my partner, John Leonard, had arrived. John looked in the suspect's driver side window and saw a fully loaded 357 Magnum on the front seat. The detective who later questioned the perpetrator told me that the "perp" admitted to them that he was "just waiting for the cop to approach" and that he was "going to shoot the cop [me] and then take off down Rt. 309 to inner city Philly." Like I said, not nearly as dramatic but certainly with the potential to be just as deadly.

Sometime around 1981, I made a personal commitment to Christ (more on that later). I began studying the Bible with the Berean Bible College of the Assemblies of God. In 1985, I began a four-year tour as the youth pastor of the Family Worship Center in Lansdale, Pa.

Working at the Family Worship Center for Pastor JR Damiani, I quickly succumbed to my own "success." JR taught me a lot and gave me many opportunities to expand my horizons and experiences for this, I will always be grateful. The life of a Christian is a journey, a journey to **learn**, to **experience**, to **change** and yes, to **make mistakes**. For the first time in my Christian walk I became the "victim" of my own success. I use the term 'victim' loosely here as I never have subscribed to the "victim mentality" promoted by liberals. **All of us must take responsibility for our own actions!**

Looking back, I can see I just was not ready for the responsibilities and the trust Pastor JR placed in me. Just like when I became a police officer at the age of 18, you could not have told me then, but I know now, I was just not ready. I did not know it at the time, but my foundations(s) were not built on Jesus Christ and Him crucified. Rather, God was getting ready to show me that my foundation(s) were being built on my "good-works and success." Without knowing it, I began straying from the Lord, however, I remained reasonably successful as the youth pastor and had a four year run at that same church. Evangelist Dave Roever once told me the average longevity for a youth pastor was somewhere in the neighborhood of 18 months; the Lord only knows what the average is today. How I wish God would have stopped my "success" back then, but He knew it would take some very tough lessons to get through my thick, pride-full skull.

Family Worship Center in Lansdale, Pa.

By my fourth year as the Youth Pastor at F.W.C., I had strayed from the Lord, and was backslidden. My role as a "Pastor" became more play acting than that of a sincere heart to serve God with proper motives. Although outside I was functioning well, my hypocrisy started to cause me great consternation, but I had no idea how to fix the problem.

All of my Christian life I have always taken the words of the Apostle Paul about Communion very seriously. In First Corinthians, Chapter eleven, Paul talks about the importance of examining yourself before you eat the bread and drink the cup of the Lord. He goes on to say that if you take Communion un-worthily you can actually die prematurely. I always pay attention to that part of the Bible, seldom referred to from pulpits today. Although I was still working for the church, I was far from God, and by now, steeped in sin, I had no idea how I had gotten there. I remember one morning service, after wrestling with my demons for weeks; I was scheduled to help serve Communion in church. I was a mental and physical wreck, feeling like the ultimate hypocrite should I perform my duties as scheduled. It may seem insignificant to you, but it meant the world to me when I prayed and asked God to "get me out of this." Leaving a side room, I met Pastor JR in the lobby and he asked me if it would be ok if one of the elders of the church stood in for me that morning. Would it be ok!?! Hallelujah, I could hardly contain myself.

Just the fact that God heard my prayer that morning and gave me an IMMIDIATE answer, led me to cry out to God for more help. I wanted out of the bondage I was in, yet I had no strength within myself to resist. Now, if you are more concerned about the specifics of my sin at that time, you'll miss the big picture here. It does not matter what sin or sins are keeping us from a full relationship with God. For some it will be drugs, for others alcohol or pornography, stealing, lying, cheating, the list goes on and on. That "thing" that "sin" that holds dominion in your life, has to go! The bible say's that if you think you do not have any sin in your life, **you are a liar!** (*More on getting rid of that "thing" in your life, in coming chapters*)

I went to a local youth center late one night. It was a converted barn where we held youth meetings. I laid on my face before God and begged him to give me the strength to resist my temptations. I knew I was wrong but still either unable or unwilling to run away from my sin as I should have. I begged God to intervene, and HE did. That week we held our usual weekly youth meeting in the same converted barn and as was usually the case, my assistant Gary McMichael was there to help. Raising my three daughters I was always very physical with them in that I would spin them around or throw them in the air for fun. I never dropped them but would often make other adults gasp at the daringness. We called it "astronaut training" and all three of my daughters never seemed to stop laughing or enjoying it. Just days earlier, as was my custom, I had thrown my 5 year old daughter Sarah in the air and realized she was growing too much for this particular activity. Gary was a great guy who had a calling on his life and was really a "Minister in Training" with me as his mentor. Gary would come over to our house often and our kids enjoyed his throwing them around just as much as they did mine. On this particular night, Gary picked Sarah up and threw her in the air. Her feet came down and hit his chest, causing her to repel away from his grasp, crashing the back of her head on the carpet covered, cement floor. All I heard was the thud". 48 hours of gut- wrenching waiting and prayer was all the motivation I needed to break the *spiritual bondage* I found myself in. I repented, and promised God I was done with that sinful behavior forever. Never once did I look back after that. Sarah later fully recovered from a fractured skull, and I kept my word to God.

Later, for reasons unrelated to my sin, or maybe because of it. The inevitable separation from the Family Worship Center came. I saw this as a chance for a fresh start, a new beginning, and so Deborah and I started the YouthQuest Evangelistic Association, YouthQuest for short. With a grand kick-off and about seventy-five dollars we set out to reach un-churched teenagers in the Philadelphia area, whatever it took – we were doing this for the Lord. By the end of our fifth year of running YouthQuest, our Board of Directors was looking at a budget of nearly $300,000 dollars. An incredible amount of "success" in a very short time – unfortunately much of it built on wood, hay, and stubble. Once again, my "foundation(s) were being built on "good-works" and "success." Rather than on, Jesus Christ and Him crucified!

By that time, I had written my second small book – which was met with moderate success. We had a cable access television show, a staff of approximately forty volunteers, a thrift store, seven part time foster homes, a twenty-four-hour emergency "hot-line." We were holding two public meetings a week with between twenty and two hundred teenagers showing up each time.

Me (left) speaking to a crowd of teens

We had two transportation vans and were providing counseling, crisis pregnancy help, foster care, and emergency food and shelter. Every Christmas we distributed hundreds of gifts to underprivileged teenagers and their families and YouthQuest became the only 'Christian' licensed foster care facility for teenagers in Pennsylvania. I was selected Grand Marshall of the Lansdale Christmas Parade and life was looking very good. I could probably write three separate books about the lives of three of the thirty-two teens Deborah and I personally took into our home. *An The Bui* – a Vietnamese child placed on a makeshift boat by his mother in South Vietnam after his Christian father was executed by Communist authorities. Or, *Jennifer* – who was being sexually abused by her deacon step-father. When we took Jennifer's side and defended her, much of the Christian community ostracized Deborah and me. Or *Sherry,* who came to us as a lice-infested twelve year old who was living in a car. Not only did Deborah have to de-louse her, she had to teach her everything about her changing body and personal hygiene. For Deborah and me this was not a "job," it was a twelve year calling. However, without realizing it, I started again to drift away from God.

Our car when Deborah and I were selected as the Grand Marshalls of the hometown Christmas Holiday Parade.

We did a lot of good and helped a lot of people; in fact, hundreds, maybe a thousand or two made professions of faith in Christ. I started to be viewed as the local "expert" in raising uncontrollable teenagers, speaking at civic clubs, television and radio appearances, churches and even having the Department of Children and Youth use my writings for some of their training. In my mind, I could do no wrong. I talked about things like the newly launched MTV phenomenon.

MTV

As a conservative, I tend to look at things in black and white. Before you shout amen, keep in mind this is the exact opposite of the world view today. Over the years they have even made a few movies about people living in a black and white world. It's not until the colors start coming out that people begin to "progress." This is why, as sold by marketing geniuses, MTV music videos had become a billion dollar industry. MTV brings the colors out!

Before I expand on that, let me give my philosophical view on this. Yes, I do think things should be looked at in black and white, right or wrong, good or bad. This is a basic Biblical principle. Because it is a principle laid down by God, the world system fights against it. This is just the natural order of things in the live or die spot we find ourselves in throughout the entire history of mankind.

Like Billy Graham said to me so many years ago, we were placed here for a purpose. Life is not the lonely journey some have made it out to be. There is a cure for sadness; there is cure for not feeling "connected." MTV & emerging social media offer impressionable young people a temporary fix to these sentiments, these sentimental feelings. This void, this emptiness, was actually placed there by God as a means to help you seek HIM out. Everyone who pays attention has those feelings to one degree or another. Every one of us has an empty feeling in us for MORE. More of what – we may not know. In the case of MTV's rock-stars, rap stars, all stars – they may try to make people THINK they know the answers to life's tough questions, but they don't. The marketing geniuses at MTV have all but completely reversed the music industry. Coupled with the introduction of ; I-pods, I-Tunes, clouds, and social media all silently pumping up our children's heads with gangster rap. Gangster Rap music feeds to the most primal instinct of young people: SEX & SELF! Some rap stars, who use the vilest lyrics, are now making millions of dollars with corporate sponsorships. Lyrics that degrade and debase women, and use streams of profanity are just now getting the attention of leaders in the black community. Where has Al Sharpton and Jesse Jackson been all these years? These "artists" are making millions through MTV marketers. But, sadly, few of them give back to the communities from which they rose. MTV is all about power and positioning. MTV is not alone; there are several other competitive music markets as well. Never was the power of MTV more obvious than in the 2004 presidential election. The MTV crowd continued its ongoing "Get out the VOTE" drive, and in 2004 many MTV moguls were convinced this was their year. Fortunately for us, they were not nearly as successful as they thought they would be. But make no mistake, they viewed that election as nothing more than an opinion poll which told them they still have a way to go. Music moguls will come back at this year after year after year. Their spokespeople will tell you that getting involved in the process is the "American way" and they are correct! What they don't tell you is that they will do everything to get young people involved in the liberal/progressive, American way. For evidence, we need only look at the jackbooted thugs who run the National Education Association with an iron fist and squash anyone or anything that disagrees with their humanistic, socialist philosophies. Our entire public education system was doomed to failure when we first allowed God to be removed and then we allowed our "educators" to concentrate on **indoctrination rather than education.** The latest educational fads such as; Agenda 21, Common core, and whatever the flavor of the year might be has one underlining purpose; make good little (obedient) citizens of our children. In their eyes, the State must be served!

When Bill Clinton first broke the barrier into the power of young people via the music video crowd, it was nothing short of genius. It remains to be seen if the timing is right for a large enough turnout to have Hillary Clinton or Barrack Obama elected as president, but bear in mind, the MTV/socialist generation has every intention of taking over politically and economically. *All that is necessary for evil to triumph....*

How many conservatives are there who are so fed up that they won't vote for anybody? This contagious disease is nearing epidemic proportions in the conservative movement. It's not too late – by large margins this country is far more conservative than it is "progressive," but our numbers are declining, while theirs are growing. Lest you think the MTV music video world is not a billion dollar business, just take a look at its incestuous business practices. They do take care of their own, whereas we conservatives have made it our life's mission to split hairs and get worked up over the most stupid things that literally keep us from working together on common causes. Time to get back into the fight, folks.

So, as an ENTIRE GENERATION is spoon fed by the likes of social and gangster rap, we need to brace ourselves for what I believe will soon be the most selfish society in the world. Face it, people only had three feelings about the war in Iraq to overthrow Saddam Hussein. They blamed President Bush for being a power hungry oil grabber; they felt we should just mind our own business and take care of ourselves; or they were in favor of the war. Almost without exception, this selfish spoon fed society was 100% against the war in Iraq. Now whether you agreed or did not agree, you'll miss the point if you worry about that. What you need to see is that an ENTIRE GENERATION is being raised by MTV – a handful of angry liberals that hate all things conservative at every level and are amassing an army of liberals that will some day VOTE. These potential voters are being spurned on by the likes of anti-American, Rosie O'Donnell. Thanks to the Rosie O'Donnell's of the world, there a so few real American hero's for our kids to look up to anymore. Decent "All-American" hero's will soon be a thing of the past. Heck, even Marvel comics which owns the rights to Captain America, "the living symbol of freedom," recently had him killed and put to rest!

In my current hometown of Tucson, Arizona, a Latino woman was giving a speech to a captive audience of public high school students when she made this incredible statement: "Remember, Republicans hate Latinos, ok? Republicans hate Latinos." This is how free the left and those who would see the United States decimated from the inside feel in their ongoing quest to indoctrinate our children into helping promote a socialist/globalist society. The myth of man made global warming is another example that could take up an entire book in this regard.

As for my five-year run of "notoriety" and "success" with YouthQuest speaking of such things like MTV, and such. The sin of PRIDE sprung it's ugly trap, without knowing it (again), I had fallen head-first into the black hole that is the sin of pride. As big as YouthQuest became, Steve Aiken's pride grew as well. Yes, the Lord used me for a time but after that, I was benched, and I mean BENCHED – big time! God is a jealous God and HE will not stand for US taking credit for HIS marvelous works. It is not unusual for a Preacher, or any Christian worker for that matter, to be "effective," even if he or she has hidden sin in their life. I think we would be shocked if we ever knew just how many are actually out there under those exact circumstances. Please don't make the mistake of thinking it is your job, or your DUTY, to expose such persons, it's not. The church has enough "splinter-picker-outers". Trust me; God does not need your help and HE will deal with them, in His time! **Numbers 32:23**

Chapter 4
FALSE CHARGES

After two trials resulted in hung juries, Roscoe (Fatty) Arbuckle was acquitted at the third, with a written apology from the jury --- an apology unprecedented in American justice. "Acquittal is not enough for Roscoe Arbuckle [they wrote]. We feel that a great injustice has been done him ... there was not the slightest proof adduced to connect him in any way with the commission of a crime. He was manly throughout the case and told a straightforward story which we all believe. We wish him success and hope that the American people will take the judgment of fourteen men and women that Roscoe Arbuckle is entirely innocent and free from all blame."

Short of losing a loved one, or some cataclysmic event or disease, I cannot think of anything worse in life than to be falsely accused of something you did not do. Figuratively speaking, God was getting ready to allow a sledge hammer to hit me in the head, to knock me off my false foundation(s) and right my motives before Him once and for all! Bear with me while I set the stage for the entire reason that led me to write this book.

At my high school in Lansdale, Pennsylvania, where I was the Senior Class President, I practically lived at my school because of all the meetings and activities I attended. It was dusk and as I approached the school building one night, I was carrying a very old-fashioned, hand-held scanner. I carried this scanner because I was still heavily involved as a volunteer ambulance and rescue worker. It's a radio receiver many ambulance and rescue members carried in case a call went out for help. Although these devices did not even come close to the communication tools of today, they had fairly good reception. I carried this little scanner with me everywhere I went. For a variety of reasons, the device did not work inside my high school. The scanner had a tiny red light on top of it so that you knew the power was on. As I approached a side door of one of the school's buildings, knowing the device would not work, I simply turned it off as I got to the door. The side door corridor I had entered had many large panes of glass that allow a person to see outside the whole time they walk this corridor. As I approached the door, assistant football coach and P.E. teacher, Ed Lugg, was walking down the glass corridor. Mr. Lugg was a Hulk-en figure and the kind of teacher and Coach NOBODY messed around with. If he had a sense of humor nobody I knew ever saw it. From a distance, he had seen the little red light on my hand from the scanner I was holding (the case was black and could not be seen at that time of night) and immediately assumed I was smoking a cigarette. Smoking in high school back then was a suspendable offense. I turned off the scanner as I entered the doorway and Coach Lugg simply assumed I had put out my cigarette before entering the building. This was a reasonable assumption given the twilight darkness and low light level at this particular entrance. The next day I was summoned to the principal's office where I was told I was being given a suspension from school for smoking on school grounds. "WHAT?" I asked aggressively. Smoking? Ask my friends, my family, I DON'T smoke cigarettes. Although many of my school friends smoked and we all engaged in an occasional marijuana joint or two, I simply have never smoked an entire cigarette in my life. In my neighborhood when I was about 11 some older teenage boys offered to let me try one of theirs. I did not like it and I have never smoked a cigarette since. Ok, some pot and an occasional cigar when I used to play poker but let's not get off track.

I insisted on seeing the principal, Mr. Matusky, personally. I was not about to have them process the paper work for my suspension without a fight! Mr. Matusky angrily escorted me into his office and was upset that I was wasting his time trying to wrangle my out of the suspension. He related the "facts" as Mr. Lugg had presented them (at that time I did not equate my little red light on top of my scanner as the culprit of my dilemma). My defense was: "I DON'T SMOKE, ASK MY FRIENDS" and a "Where is the cigarette butt, the evidence?" thrown in. Mr. Matusky thought for a second and decided to grant me a reprieve not because he believed me, but because Mr. Lugg had not followed procedure by confronting me immediately and securing the evidence. I was a free man. It was not until weeks later, while entering the building at night again and turning off my scanner as I had done previously that it occurred to me what Mr. Lugg thought he witnessed. It was that incident that made me seriously consider becoming a defense attorney. Since then I have read several studies about just how unreliable eye witnesses can be. Any decent cop will tell you, that although an eye witness can make a compelling argument for what they saw or think they saw, the witnesses can sometimes be completely wrong when they convey their account.

The Sledge Hammer!

My whole world came crashing down one day in 1995 when I received a phone call from a police detective to come down to the precinct station. In my work with YouthQuest as a youth worker and former police officer, it was common to deal with the police on a regular basis. Youth crime, runaway kids, assaults, theft – you name it – I dealt with it and teenagers at one time or another. We were a full service, non-profit organization bent on helping homeless and troubled teenagers. This call from the detective was different, however, and you can't begin to realize the absolute horror and shock I felt when I found out two teenage girls had accused me of "inappropriate behavior" – essentially of having an affair with them.

Both of these girls had been treated as members of our family. One of them lived with us for many months, as one of 32 foster children my wife and I took into our home for various periods of time. The other was at our house as much, if not more, than my own daughters. Running a mission for homeless teenagers is not a nine to five job. It was 24 hours a day, seven days a week.

In writing this book, I debated back and forth whether I should go into explicit details about the specific charges against me, narrow down each piece of "evidence," and defend myself at each turn. Or, simply state the facts and continue writing about the incredible life lessons the Lord was teaching me through HIS "breaking process" to refine and humble me, to make me a better man. I chose the latter.

After being falsely accused and spending 74 days in jail for a crime I did not commit, I fell SO far from God, angry and bitter at Him for allowing this to happen. I did not think I would ever get back to my relationship with HIM. Just the charges alone put me on the front page of every newspaper within a 50 mile radius of my hometown, as well as the lead story for all local news channels. That night.

I climbed inside a bottle of booze and did not come out for almost five years. Self-medicating, I took every pill, smoked every joint, and engaged in every type of sinful behavior I could think of. Of course, I lost my position as executive director and my only source of income. More anger and bitterness grew dispapotionetley and drove me further from God. With no job and no viable means of support, to a small degree I got involved with low level "connected" street thugs from a Philadelphia crime family just earn a little cash. I ended up getting arrested twice. Thank God I never killed anyone or got killed myself. I was so spiritually dead, I don't think I would be here today if the Lord had not carried me back to safety, back to healing **and YES, rescued me**!

You may identify with what I am saying because you are somewhat off course yourself. Now is the time to give up your survival instincts and just allow God to direct your paths, only then can He rescue you!

For this very reason, make every effort to add to your faith goodness; and to goodness, knowledge; and to knowledge, self-control; and to self-control, perseverance; and to perseverance, godliness; and to godliness, brotherly kindness; and to brotherly kindness, love. For if you possess these qualities in increasing measure, they will keep you from being ineffective and unproductive in your knowledge of our Lord Jesus Christ. **2 Peter 1:5-8**

If you are reading this and want to know how to get back, make up your mind to start today, not tomorrow or in a few weeks when you feel better, make up your mind to start TODAY! Realize, everyone has a "sinful nature;" a preponderance to lean towards sin. Our "Adamic-nature" is only countered by the power of Christ's death, burial, and resurrection! March forward by placing your faith only in the cross of Jesus Christ, follow orders, and trust that HE will direct your paths – HE WILL! Even if He makes you go all the way back to basic training boot camp, as He did me. God's breaking process hurts. If you are determined to be the man or women God intends you to be, it will not be easy. If it were easy, everybody would do it! Don't get me wrong, no human effort of any kind takes the place of the sacrifice Jesus paid for you at the cross. However, the decision to kneel at the foot of that cross begins with you saying; "yes" to the Lord!

Many "Christians" today make the mistake of thinking their "salvation experience" is sufficient for all time. They have gladly received the gift of God's grace, but have refused to make Jesus, Lord of their lives. That was me back then. I heard Pastor Adrian Rogers once compare this type of religious experience to a newlywed couple: Sue and Bill just married in the church. The rice and the bouquet have been thrown, both Bill and Sue are in the car being driven off to start their new life together. In the back seat of the car Sue turns to Bill and say's that was a beautiful wedding, the most heart felt experience of my life, thank you, now take me home to my mother! What, Bill asks, what in the world do mean? Sue explains to Bill; yes, I married you but you can't expect me to change my life. I'll see you on the weekends (especially on Sunday's and Holiday's). You are my husband and I expect you to provide for me and protect me, but don't expect me to change anything in my life. If I need money or anything else, I'll be sure to come to you and ask for it, but that is as far as I am willing to go.

This is how many of us approach our Christianity, I sure did. Enjoying all the benefits of this "marriage" but never really making Jesus the Lord of my life. In order to fully follow Christ and make Him Lord of our lives, we must take ourselves down from the thrown of our lives and realize it is no longer our own, Jesus must sit on the thrown of your life in order to truly call Him Lord!

    As successful as I was growing up – former police officer, nationally known bodyguard, featured in countless newspaper articles, Grand Marshall of my hometown

Christmas Parade, my own cable access television show – it was as if almost everything I ever touched turned to gold. Because the Lord cares about me, he allowed me to get "whacked" with this experience for my own good. My heart and my motives had grown so far from my Christianity, I remember recognizing my sin and crying out to Him again to right the wrongs in my heart – "whatever it takes." For everything I had to go through to get to this point in my life, I am eternally grateful. According to the Bible I am not an illegitimate "child of God." If I were, I probably would have continued my "scorched earth" policy as it relates to others and subsequently, probably, and deservedly, ended up dead and in Hell where I belonged.

But God is good!

Two teenage girls, Melody and Harriet (not their real names), with the help of a "Christian counselor" we'll call Barry, got together and accused me of being inappropriate with them. Barry did everything within his power to destroy me and the YouthQuest ministry we had built. He was running his own "youth program" at the time. Barry saw himself in competition with me. Later Deborah would attribute his harmful behavior to pure jealousy!

As an aside years later, Barry was later jailed for drugging one of the young women who had accused me falsely. Barry was convicted of attempting to rape her while she was unconscious. He pled guilty and was sentenced to 11 and a half to 23 months in prison. This is the level of evil both Deborah and I were contending with, not just with Barry, but with many others who were determined to crush and destroy us. It took me almost ten years to forgive Barry, but I finally did, I do pray for him as well as the two girls from time to time. To the Christian, forgiveness is not an option! I can never expect to be forgiven if I am unwilling to forgive. Remember, ***Obedience is better than sacrifice.***

With all due respect for people who have been disfigured or disabled due to accident or injury. I can tell you with all authority, the only "heart pain" worse than what Deborah and I went through would be the death of a loved one. Short of that "death" there is NOTHING worse somebody can go through in life than being **falsely accused** of sexual assault or inappropriateness; in my case, a 17 and an 18 year old girl.

This nightmare began with us taking Melody into our home. What a neglected life this girl had experienced. At age 15, after being abandoned by her mother and father, Melody gave birth to a baby girl that she decided to keep and raise on her own. After many placements in and around the county, Melody came to us. She became the 32nd foster child Deborah and I took into our own home over a period of many years. Melody was 17 years old when we took in her and her two year old daughter. In hindsight, this was a horrible mistake. Not only had Melody accused two other men of abusing her in similar fashion in previous placements, but having her live in our home when our oldest daughter Mindy needed more of her parents' attention was detrimental to all of our children's development and well being, especially Mindy's. At that point in my life I deserved an "F" as a father and another "F" at being a husband. Like many fathers I have talked to, I was far too strict with my oldest daughter. My outbursts of anger at home and my selfishness about life in general was not consistent with what God required of me. I made Mindy's life much more miserable than it needed to be. Although Mindy and I do not talk much, later in life, (for the most part,) we I worked things out and she turned out to be a good Christian women and caring mom. How can we correct the mistakes of the past in raising our children? I have learned that three crucial words go miles in helping our children come to grips with the many, many mistakes we parents all make raising them. What can any of us say to our children for the mistakes we made raising them? "I am sorry" are words probably 95% of the moms and dads reading this need to say to their children from time to time.

    The second and perhaps more critical thing that parents must remember in raising children is this: We CANNOT expect the church or the youth Pastor or the Christian school to be responsible for whether or not our children mature as Christian adults. You are fooling yourself if you think you can just dump the responsibility you have as a parent onto an organization, school or church. We just now are starting to see in society the devastating effects of children being raised by the state in day-care, pre-school, and high schools. These children are growing up and sometimes will do ANYTHING for attention, to be noticed, to be loved. Although Deborah and I sacrificed financially, we were determined for her to stay home while our daughters were young and often did "without" as a result.

    Third and finally, it's nonsense to act one way in church or in public and another way at home. This is called **hypocrisy,** and our children not only see right through it, they suffer long term hurt by it's mixed message. It's a sad truth, but many in church LEADERSHIP today are doing just that. Do you do things and say things at home that you would never do or say at church? I sure did. If your answer is "yes", you already have a problem, recognize it and get busy getting better. The Lord will help you if you ask him to.

    There is no crime in being human and making mistakes. Admitting them, asking for forgiveness, and changing the behavior are infinitely healthier in the long-run than simply shrugging our shoulders and never addressing problems at all. Remember, **growing as a Christian is not about being "good", it's about being "better."** Deborah and I are now very blessed to have three grown daughters who, (for the most part) are living for the Lord and turned out pretty OK.

Sadly, some children will not forgive their parents and some parents will never forgive their children. We are only responsible for our own behavior, not how others react or fail to react to our attempt to make amends. Never think that just saying empty words will resolve past sins: they won't. However, as we grow and learn from our mistakes and learn what "amazing grace" is all about, that will go many miles toward helping you get healed and whole.

For a many reasons, having Melody live in our house was a very bad thing. No, I did not have sex with her. Eventually though I used egregiously bad judgment as many of my "talks" with Melody became too personal and inappropriate. Having said that, yes, of course it was SIN! Sin that was eating at me, I turned to the only person in the world I trusted, my wife Deborah. Although I downplayed to Deborah the depth of the adrenaline rush I was experiencing having an attractive young woman look up to me for advice, I did confide in her about the struggle I was having with Melody living in our house. Knowingly or unknowingly, Melody's behavior at home became more and more suggestive as well. She would make inappropriate comments, or she would adjust her clothing seductively when Deborah was not around. As Melody's behavior became increasingly more inappropriate, Deborah finally put her foot down and demanded that I go and "talk to somebody," but to whom? I had seen enough confidences broken and enough betrayal in churches to last a lifetime, whom could I trust? I chose a Christian psychologist, Dr. Reilly (*not his real name*) who told me after our very first meeting; "Melody had to go" – but where?

Of course Melody, having become a part of our family, felt incredibly betrayed. When Melody left us, she started seeing her new "counselor" Barry. Barry was only too happy to take on the case of a teenager that my program or I had failed. It was just a matter of days before Melody made similar claims about me as she had done in two previous foster home settings. Barry encouraged Melody to go to the police. To this day, my wife Deborah swears Barry's motives were nothing more than evil jealousy. She related to me how, for years, whenever I was not around, Barry would "hit" on her. I tend to think my wife was right about the whole "jealousy" thing. Deborah even captured Barry on video when he arrived at the grocery store where she worked. Although Barry was married, he was harassing Deborah and asking her to leave me for him. What a guy Barry was!

Years earlier, and prior to all this, Barry and I parted ways when I became very critical of his methods of "ministry." After getting his degree in nursing, he began working with teenagers at a mental health clinic. On several occasions, I was quoted as saying that Barry was "prostituting" himself by keeping kids in a "program" and collecting insurance payments for his services all while calling it "ministry." Where is the motivation to graduate a teen from your program if you continue to receive fees from insurance carriers? In my opinion, if you are paid to help someone, there is no motivation to help that person get well as long as you keep receiving funds for the individual "help" you are giving. **It is not "ministry" if you are charging a fee!** At YouthQuest we never charged a dime for our services. Hundreds of teens were helped by understanding their problems in relationship to the Word of God. In short, we got kids saved and plugged them into local churches for follow up. We were a "faith based program" before faith based programs were cool. None of it would have been possible without private donations from individuals and churches who believed in what we were accomplishing. Teens that needed more from mental health professionals were referred to a network of Christian counselors (not Barry) and often times YouthQuest would pay the bills.

Barry was one of these guys who graduated from Teen Challenge; he was sent there on his third DUI and then said he had "repented." The problem was, when Barry "repented" he somehow got it in his head that he knew more than anybody else about Christianity, the Bible, and how Christians should be living their lives. All Barry really did was get better and better at hiding his secret sins. Not unlike me when I worked at the Family Worship Center, pride will ruin you quicker than anything I know. Not only was I publicly critical of Barry, a lot of people in town did not know he and his family lived directly above us for about two years. His wife, Judy (*not her real name*), and Deborah were very good friends. I remember Barry sitting in my living room with tears in his eyes, telling me he thought "God wanted" us to work together in ministry, a notion I flatly rejected. After all if; "God wanted" me to work with this man, would not God Himself let me know? Another blow to Barry's ego?

Barry, who later became the prosecution's star witness against me, originally encouraged Melody (then 19) to file charges against me for allegedly touching her breast against her will. The local police Chief was quoted in the newspaper, saying; "We are looking into just how many teenage girls were victims of Mr. Aiken." Oh brother, why don't you just get a rope and find the nearest tree? It was then that Harriet, (*not her real name*) told the police she and I had a "consensual affair" when she was 17.

So, here we go again – nightmare at Steve's house, Part II. I was accused of having "consensual sex" – this time with Harriet. She told the police that she and I were lovers like Joey Buttafucco and Amy Fisher (still somewhat famous at the time). She told the police and testified that she and I had a "consensual" affair and that she was 17 at the time. She said that she and I engaged in "consensual" sex over the course of several months.

None of that is true, and I'm not speaking *a la* "Bill Clinton" – it simply is not the truth. Harriet (now in her 30s) was a very disturbed young lady who suffered the most horrible kinds of sexual abuse when she was a child. Harriet was diagnosed with Multiple Personality Disorder (MPD), now referred to as Disassociative Identity Disorder.

So why did she lie about me?

I had expelled Harriet from YouthQuest for drug use and sexual contact with a teenage boy who was also enrolled in the YouthQuest program. As a matter of fact, I had caught Harriet with a set of "works" used for "shooting up" drugs while attending one of our meetings. This was the last straw in a string of rule violations for which Harriet was famous. I explained to her that she needed more help than our "voluntary" program could offer. I also told Harriet that if she completed a residential program for her behavior and drug problems we would accept her back into YouthQuest. Harriet's reaction was somewhat typical for a teenager except…she threatened me that if I did not allow her to stay at YouthQuest, she would tell everyone that she and I had an affair. As a former cop, I am used to idle threats and treated her threats in much the same manner as I did anything else. I did tell Deborah about the threats but I was hardly concerned.

When Harriet was in our program, I was the one taking her to group meetings held by a psychologist, Tom Brownback, still practicing in Allentown, Pennsylvania. In these group meetings, Harriet was encouraged to speak freely about ANYTHING and EVERYTHING. If Harriet and I were having an affair, Tom Brownback concluded that he was certain she would have brought it up to him or the "group" at some time. She never did.

My biggest mistake with Harriet was transporting her to various mental health facilities and becoming her "taxi" the many times she ran away from home. This made it easy for suspicious observers to see the time Harriet and I spent together and conclude that an "affair" could be taking place. Although I was warned by one local pastor that I was spending too much time with Harriet, I dismissed the innuendo only because I knew, (or at least believed), the greater good was being served. What a prideful fool I was. It did not help matters that I was personally drifting even further from God at that time, all while Harriet's millionaire mother made donations to our ministry.

Think I sold out? I sure did!

Not long after this, Harriet began attending Barry's "counseling" sessions as they were forming a "support group" for all my alleged victims. This was extremely nauseating to Deborah and me given the severity of the charges. Eventually the police questioned all the teenage girls they could find and interrogated them about the times they may have been alone with me, counseling. Keep in mind that I am grateful now that the Lord took time to allow these terrible situations to come into my life. You could not tell me then, but without these horrible days and the lessons learned, I would not be the person I am today.

So, as God would have it, it was not a foreign enemy He used to bring about my personal destruction for re-molding and shaping, it was someone who was SUPPOSED to be my "brother."

But I want you to know, brethren, that the things which happened to me have actually turned out for the furtherance of the gospel; **Philippians 1:12**

You will find out that as you get knocked around in life, most of the time it is not strangers but the people closest to you who inflict the most damage. In addition to Barry, I was shocked and amazed to discover the depth of hatred the district attorney and government agents have for Christian programs. As well as a deep seated hatred for all things Christian, "Christ-a-phobia" is alive and well in government! I was the perfect target as even back then I was heavily involved in politics for the "Christian-Right."

Some months later when my cases finally went to trial, the trial judge refused to allow the jury to hear that Melody had a history of claiming sexual abuse in the two previous placements she had been in. At worst, I was guilty of talking about things I had no business discussing with her! The flirtatious bantering and the inappropriate joking around was wrong, it boggles my mind to think how far I allowed myself to get swept up, but what I did, was certainly not against the law! As my trial rolled around, I was arrogant enough to think that there was no way I could be found guilty – after all, I simply did not do the things of which I was accused. My attorney received an offer to plea bargain down to one misdemeanor, with mandatory counseling, and two years probation, no jail time. I flatly refused. It was then that the district attorney took the unprecedented step of making a motion to try the two cases together at the same time. Even though the cases were dissimilar with one girl claiming I touched her against her will and the other girl claiming that we had a consensual affair, a county judge allowed both cases to be combined – practically guaranteeing a guilty verdict of one sort or another for the DA..

Although Melody testified at my trial that she was "very frightened of me" and that the whole time she lived at our house she avoided me and "always left the room if I entered," this was a blatant lie. We tried to enter home videos of Melody interacting with all of us and especially many scenes in the video where she sat as close to me as she possibly could; however, for whatever reason, the judge did not allow us to show the video tape to the jury.

As I wrote earlier, there is no doubt that my "friendship" with Melody became inappropriate. I admitted step by step, in-depth details, to several local pastors, my wife, and the Lord, in short, I let my guard down. To this day I have no idea why I felt the need for affirmation of this nature or how I could have allowed myself to enjoy that adrenaline rush, to enter that slippery slope, but I did. Yes, it was sin! I messed up and I take full responsibility for that. How else do we learn except by example? At the time I was out of balance and I needed help. You may be feeling the same way.

As I said earlier, Dr. Reilly told me that Melody must be removed from our house, but where? At one time Melody and her baby had lived in a car. How could we just kick her out on the street when she literally had become a member of our family? I pulled in every favor I could to try and get Melody suitable housing so she could leave our home. With the help of two very godly women, Gwen Racz and Jill Shannon, we got Melody "bumped up" the line to a "Christian" housing project run by the Mennonite church.

Well, maybe not "bumped up," but we sure worked hard to get her housing fast. Throughout my trial the D.A. kept insisting that I was doing all I could to keep her in our home. It was a lie but repeated so often, I'm sure the jury believed it.

Learning she had to leave caused Melody to go into an emotional tailspin. She was rejected and angry, but she had to go! Weeks after she finally left our home, she started seeing Barry and the rest (as they say) is history. The last I heard, Melody is still living in that complex, still collecting welfare, and Barry's wife divorced him while he sat in jail. My actual offense was against my wife, my family and the God I was supposed to be serving – and He used secular means to bring about my healing through punishment!

Hundred of letters of support came pouring in and dozens of good folks lined the hallways of the courtroom, hoping to be character witnesses on my behalf. Earlier, when I was first charged, Deborah and I broke the news to Dr. Tim and Beverly LaHaye. The LaHayes were so kind, kneeling at their coffee table, they offered up prayers for us and gave Deborah and me comfort beyond words.

How morally wrong can a guy be – especially a man in my position? I died a thousands deaths over this. It never ceases to amaze me how a man can do so much good and yet sometimes if he, like me, gets off course, make such critical errors in his life. Take the case of King David, for example. I know guys like Jimmy Swaggart and thousands of others like me have used "David" as an example of human frailty and failure. Someone once said the line between good and evil runs down the middle of every man's heart.

As a boy, David was so close to God that God gave him the strength and the courage to kill a lion, a bear, and let's not forget Goliath – whom he slew with a stone and a slingshot. Yet, when David was older (wiser?) – when David was King – he fell for another man's wife. Not only did he fall for her, he arranged for her husband, Uriah, to be killed. Scoffers may say using David as an example is a total cop out. With all his failings, King David was a "man after God's own heart." He was a real man; are we not remiss if we refuse to EVER use him as an example just because he messed up? David suffered horribly for his sins. The Bible says if you are not chastened by God it is because you are not really one of His. **Hebrews 12:8** I can assure you David was one of God's own.

As I said earlier, however, I am most blessed. I have accepted the forgiveness only found in Christ. Some may roll their eyes when they hear that. How others judge you is between them and God; personally, I fear no man's condemnation.

The trial judge's refusal to allow us to bring Melody's past false claims before the jury, and combining both cases into one trial, doomed me to a guilty verdict of one form or another. These facts became some of the bases for my eventual appeals. Without regard for the plights of actual victims, Melody lived for the attention she got – at the expense of untold harm for real victims, not to mention the three families she almost destroyed. In my case the local police were more than happy to grab the headlines they got from Melody's story and my subsequent arrest: front page news like I had never seen in my hometown! Later that year, my local newspaper listed me as one of the top ten stories of the year. I may have even made number one? It was during this time that I must have watched the movie "My Cousin Vinny" over two hundred times! A tragic comedy based on a true story about some kids falsely accused of murder.

Under strict orders from my attorney, I stopped making any comments to the newspapers. This was a tough pill to swallow as it literally got to the point that when I would refuse to comment, local newspapers would run rumors and innuendo as if they were factual. One reporter even told me, "Well, if you are not going to comment then what I heard must be true." That inability to correct the "record" came back to bite me in 2006 and no doubt, will do so repeatedly. Spurious newspaper articles will probably continue to do so as long as I maintain a public persona of any kind. At any rate, after not commenting, inevitably the next day – BAM – there would be some type of juicy tidbit plastered on the front page as if it were substantiated fact! As hard as the police and newspapers dug, every teenager they questioned, both male and female, stood up for me and told the police they did not believe the stories about me were true. Several of the teenagers even told the authorities that they personally knew the two girls who were falsely accusing me and that they believed both of the girls to be habitual liars. One teenage girl that I also spent a lot of time with, was an attractive young girl named Wanda Chandler, now Wanda Alderfer, *(Wanda gave me permission to use her real name).* Wanda told Deborah and me that at one point a detective was badgering her to come up with something that they could use against me, anything! She said it was obvious they were on a witch hunt (my words not hers). The list went on and on.

All in all, about 40 teenage girls and about a dozen teenage boys were questioned and pressed hard for any sliver of evidence that might show a preponderance towards this type of behavior. I'm told most of the kids (both former and at the time current teens in our program) stood up for me, telling authorities that I never used bad language, told dirty jokes, or even gave a hint that I was inappropriate in any way. To this day, I don't tell dirty jokes, I don't talk about women's anatomy, or do any number of things that would be associated with deviant behavior. I have never been to a strip club, never entered an adult book store or a pornography place. I'm not saying this to demean those who have; I just never did. If my wife Deborah ever thought I had an attraction to teenage girls, I think the only question she would ask is; *how do you put more bullets in this gun?* I'd be a dead man! Yet try as they did, it was more important for the police and the district attorney to believe these two troubled girls than it was to believe me. When my attorney offered that I would take a lie detector test and he would even let the police administer it, the police flatly refused. We went out and had our own polygraph tests done and I passed. People who knew me and did not want to believe these allegations were true were understandably troubled by the inordinate amount of time I spent with Harriet. Much of that time included being at my house with my family. Even Harriet's mother, Joan (not her real name) admitted to several people that she checked up on us (Harriet and me) on several occasions, eavesdropping on our conversations when Harriet and I were together counseling. She made a point of telling many people that, either through a private investigator or her own sleuthing, she was very satisfied that nothing short of counseling, Bible study, and prayer was taking place between Harriet and me. For the time-line's sake, keep in mind, neither Harriet nor Melody got the police involved at all until both had been out of YouthQuest for several months.

    Now it has been many, many, years since this took place. Looking back, I ask myself why a 35-year old man would spend that much time with a teenage girl (Harriet). Of course it gave the appearance of looking bad but I had absolutely no fear. I'm not trying to justify my fascination with Harriet's psychological pathology, however I do think that anyone who has done work with "multiples" would conclude the same thing – they are fascinating case studies. Would I do it again? Not so much. But that was the extent of my involvement with her. I was not one bit attracted to the pimple-faced young lady. It was almost nauseating to think that people could actually think it was true, but what are you going to do? Harriet's mother was the only one to speak out against me at my sentencing hearing and of course to her, I was the devil incarnate. Harriet's stepfather, a former teacher who was also accused of inappropriateness with a young girl years earlier on a swing, got up on the stand and lied about his own experience. His disdain of me stemmed from the fact that Harriet flaunted my ability to make peace in their house with Harriet when he was unable to do the same thing himself. Harriet wanted everyone who would listen to believe that she and I had a full-blown, ongoing sexual relationship. **Thank God** I was born with a reasonably prominent birth mark and this is the kind of thing only sexual partners or guys in the locker room could ever know about me. To this day, Harriet cannot describe that mark, because she has never been near it or seen it. If you ever saw the movie "Identity," that specific movie comes as close to describing what was taking place with Harriet than any words I could use. I was fascinated by knowing she was the real deal – she had been diagnosed by two licensed professionals as having multiple personalities. Harriet's mom at one time offered Deborah a substantial amount of money to leave me, she said she "felt sorry" for Deborah. Now keep in mind, Joan claims to be a Christian. Once again, we shoot our wounded and those closest to us are the ones who normally hurt us the most. People still place big red letters on others regardless of the truthfulness of the allegations. If you have a big red letter on your chest for whatever reason, earned or not, please know – there is hope and healing to be found. Like with me, they may never send a rescue party. Take comfort in what the old preacher said – if you take one step towards the Lord, He'll take three towards you! Hang in there, it does get better.

My trial lasted five days. Thank God, the much more serious, sexual charges, were thrown out, thanks to the testimony of some very good friends who contradicted some of the lies Melody and Harriet told on the stand. I was, however, found guilty of "corrupting a minor," a misdemeanor (the same charge at least one parent gets every year at graduation time for having parties with high school kids and giving them beer or drinks with alcohol). Through much of the local Christian community, there arose the erroneous assumption that my actual guilt or innocence before God was predicated on the verdict of the jury. When I was found guilty, friends ran from Deborah and me, and hid from us in droves. Unfortunately, for me, God used the absolute most horrible four years of my life to accomplish HIS purpose in me and bring about the changes HE knew I needed. Sledge hammers hurt!

Years later, a friend of ours interviewed one of the jury members (an elderly Christian man) who stated that it was a "compromise verdict" in that two women on the jury had made up their minds about my guilt even before they walked into the deliberation room. Fortunately, for me the other jurors were not so quick to condemn me. Judge Smythe of Montgomery County, PA, sentenced me to 90 days in jail and my lawyers took up an immediate appeal. 90 days in jail for a misdemeanor! Under normal conditions and absent all the publicity, this charge would normally carry a $500 fine.

Like those two women jurors, maybe you are reading this and saying 'I wish you had been put away for life.' I cannot help it if you feel that way; obviously I am not as perfect as you. I will tell you the Lord was still protecting me even though by now I had surrendered to the enemy and had no spiritual life of which to speak, I was completely backslidden. My self-medicating was chronic at that point. I stayed on booze, pills, marijuana, and anything else I could get my hands on and I did not come out for almost five years, but God does know what He is doing!

About two years after my trial, Deborah and I ran into Harriet at the Union National Bank in Souderton, Pennsylvania, and she seemed shocked to see us. At that time she apologized, stating, teary-eyed – "you lost everything." Deborah and I have completely forgiven her, she's actually a good kid with a good heart. Keep in mind, I always believed I got what I deserved from God for my sin of pride. HOWEVER, when we asked Harriet to tell the police the truth, she said, "I can't, they said they would press charges against me for filing a false report if I change my story." Some system of justice! It took me many years to finally forgive Harriet, her mom, Barry and all those involved, but forgive them I truly have. Unless we are willing to forgive, my Bible tells me it is impossible to be forgiven, and, oh, how we all need the forgiveness of God. If you are harboring un-forgiveness towards anyone for anything, you are hurting yourself more than anyone else is. Like a cancer, un-forgiveness will eat away at your soul!

Chapter 5
FROM BAD TO WORSE

Since I had no money at all, I borrowed money from my mother's retirement fund to take up my appeal. The appeals for my conviction lasted about two years. First, the Superior Court ruled against me in a written decision that made my new lawyer wonder if the court were actually even talking about my specific case. It seemed that its reasoning for refusing my appeal had little if any bearing on my case or the merits thereof. Although I was technically correct through the law, I was still trying to run from God's correction. Big mistake; just ask Jonah.

I took my appeal to the Pennsylvania Supreme Court. I was so convinced that I could win at that level, I began to struggle to put my life back together again. It seemed like every time I would start to get back on my feet, a ruling would be handed down or something would happen that would put my picture back in the newspaper and I would either get fired from a job or not get hired at all. We were broke, hungry, and losing everything. By then, to all of us, it looked like nobody on the planet gave a damn.

These were by far the hardest times for my family and me. How Deborah stuck by me is beyond my comprehension. Many of our "friends" were advising her to leave me. Many times we had no money for groceries. By now my house was in foreclosure; our electric and water had been shut off on several occasions and the unpaid bills seemed to know no end. I was getting angrier and angrier. Deborah and I wanted to file for bankruptcy but we could not even afford to do that – now that's a Catch 22. I can't tell you how many different ways I thought about getting even with Barry and "getting back" at him for causing my family so much pain. I would lie in bed at night and plan ways to hurt him without getting caught. I was fixated and it was getting dangerous. I began to supplement my heavy drinking with heavy duty narcotic pain pills: Percocet, Vicodin, OxyContin – ANYTHING that was available on the street.

So few Christians kept any kind of contact with me at all during those years and this only added to my bitterness and anger. Without a steady income, I started collecting debts for unsavory characters in and around Philadelphia. I would do these "favors" for low-level loan sharks connected with crime families in return for some money and drugs. After all, I still had my strength and my martial arts training. I'm not proud of the scare tactics and threats of violence I used and I'm just grateful I never killed anybody. This is a horrible way to live your life, especially if you are running from God. I justified my actions by telling myself; I had to support my family.

Although I lied through my teeth to get the job, I did finally land a decent job as a salesperson at Circuit City and left inner city Philadelphia once and for all. Once I got the job at Circuit City, I stayed clean and sober for almost eight months without any programs or counseling. I actually had some hope restored and it was all I apparently needed to clean up. Was I cured?

That brings us to March 13, 1998. I was coming home from work at Circuit City about ten at night, taking a major highway, Rte. 309. A teenage girl (coincidence?) crashed into me at 73 mph while I was stopped at a red light. She and her friends were driving north on Rte. 309 neck and neck – speeding up, slowing down, laughing at each other, and hogging both northbound lanes. By the time she looked up and saw me stopped at the red light, it was too late. She walked away from the accident and I was taken to the nearest trauma unit, Abington Hospital. All I really remember about the accident is a woman climbing in the car with me (I'm pretty sure she said she was a nurse) and a police officer leaning in my car and asking the rescue squad, "Is this one going by helicopter?" I must have been a pretty terrible patient as one doctor began to prepare me for the famous "halo." "YOU'RE GOING TO DRILL HOLES IN MY WHAT!!!!" I don't think so!!!! Holes in my head for many weeks just to hold my skull in place? Just give me some pills and help me out of here! I was pretty insistent that I wanted to "sign myself out" of the hospital at that point but the doctors credited my behavior to a head injury and would not give me the opportunity to do so.

  As we do today, we had an unlisted phone number and my poor wife was home that night, extremely sick with the flu. It was not until about 2:00 a.m. that the police dispatcher got through to Deborah, only telling her that there was a horrible accident and she was needed at the Abington Hospital immediately. When Deborah asked if I was dead or alive, the dispatcher refused to answer, telling Deborah she needed to go immediately! Fearing the worst, Deborah dragged herself out of her own "death-bed" and made the 30-minute trip to Abington.

  Knowing fully well that they would either have to sedate me or tie me down to fit me for the halo, I can only believe that God himself sent the nicest nurse I have EVER met in my life to my bedside. She held my hand and tried to calm me down before she had to start shaving my head. Because she was so nice, I quietly asked her if I wasn't at least entitled to a "second-opinion." As she started to say, "Not at this late hour…" she stopped herself and said, "I'll be right back." Less than five minutes later she came back with a young surgeon in tow. She told the doctor I did not want the halo and in fact, I wanted to sign myself out AMA (Against Medical Advice). The surgeon held up my X-ray, looked at it, looked at me and then looked at the X-ray again. He said, "You really don't want this thing, do you?" Of course I did not hesitate to say no. This unknown doctor then flipped the X-ray onto my chest and said "hard collar." I realized he was referring to a neck brace –which I ended up wearing for many months.

Just as Deborah arrived, I was taken to a private room and we were told that I had fractured my C-5 vertebra and that, although the prognosis was good (I could move all my body parts), they prepared me for a long rehabilitation. Adding insult to injury, I was also told that I would probably never be playing racquetball again. By then I was earning a few dollars in racquetball through tournaments and giving lessons. Although those of us who played on the "circuit" did it for the fun, we were definitely in the "minor leagues" – not quite as good as the pros but having a lot of fun, weekend after weekend. Semi-professional racquetball had become my staple, my way of life for a while. Hearing that I could never play racquetball again was not information I was going to receive well. As they say, "denial is not just a river in Egypt."

Deborah went home soon after only to have our van break down. She had to wake our friend and closest neighbor, Karen Wright, to come and get her. Still in the hospital the next day, I waited until the nurses changed shifts at three o'clock in the afternoon and I literally escaped! – down the fire escape and out a side door, neck brace and all. I spent the rest of 1998 in physical rehabilitation and back on those cursed pain pills. Instead of treating me, I found doctor after doctor who would prescribe Percocet or OxyContin like they were handing out candy. I went right back to drinking heavily, smoking marijuana, and often mixing the alcohol with the narcotics. I was oblivious to life.

During this time, my "injury lawyer" was advising me to stay in a wheelchair and let him "handle everything." I was not about to play the invalid for a chance at some big payout. Between Pennsylvania's no fault laws and my refusal to stay bed-ridden, we never sued anybody for my accident and never received a dime. My unpaid medical bills from the broken neck and other expenses exceeded $265,000.00. An awful lot of money back then.

The appeal of my case was taken to the Pennsylvania Supreme Court which refused to hear it. I still believe that if the PA Supreme Court had taken up my appeal, I would have finally been vindicated, wishful thinking perhaps. For many years I had a federal appeal winding its way through the court system. However, eventually I ran out of any money to pay lawyers and so, that was that.

Not that I speak from want: for I have learned, in whatever state I am, to be content. I know how to be without, and I know how to be with plenty: everywhere and in all things I am instructed both to be full and to be hungry, both to have plenty and to suffer need. I can do all things through Christ who strengthens me. **Philippians 4:11-13**

So with a broken neck, unable to work, unable to do very much except read, I decided to get it over with and serve my 90 day sentence. After all, what did I have to lose? I could have stayed out of jail while my federal appeal was pending. The tortuous thought of having to go to jail if I lost my appeal after I started a new life, however, seemed way too disruptive. Deep down, I also knew it was the only way I was going to get clean and sober again. Unlike most who were watching, when I saw Martha Stewart's press conference years later, I identified with her plight. I decided to call my then attorney, Harvey Sernovitz, and asked him to make arrangements for me to turn myself in, neck brace and all.

On 'the day,' our friend Fred Tarsitano drove Deborah and me to the courthouse. I had taken a fist full of painkillers and was a walking zombie. I walked into the courtroom and as I suspected, several reporters were there, waiting for me. I don't think I made any comment; I was too preoccupied with being handcuffed and whisked away to the holding cells downstairs. My, how times had changed – I actually remembered locking people up in this very same manner. The scariest time I had was on the bus ride over from the courthouse to the jail. I sat next to this man, probably in his late 30s, and he asked me where I was from. When I told him Lansdale he said, "Did you know Bobby Nester?" "Whoa! Bobby Nester? – Dead Bobby Nester?"

The man told me Nester killed himself at Camp Hill Prison. I already knew that from many years ago. I'm talking WAY BACK! When I was in 9th grade, Bobby and I had gotten in a fight in the men's room at school. He ended up a bloody mess, unconscious on the floor, and I ended up with a broken thumb, having missed his head with a punch when he went limp and then punching my hardest into the corner of the walls….ouch.

But just the fact that this convict was able to put me with Bobby Nester made me very concerned about having three strikes against me. Strike one: former cop. Strike two: former minister. Strike three: accused of a sex crime.

Falsely accused, wrongfully convicted, it makes no difference inside those walls – YOU ARE GUILTY!

After going through the normal processing – you may not appreciate it, but I sure did – somehow the Lord let me get out of the customary strip search. To this day I do not know how except I can only assume that when the guard left me for a few minutes and then came back, the processing guard thought the search had already been done. I'm sure most of you would understand that there was no way I was going to remind him. Can you imagine that? Hey officer – by the way, you forgot to strip-search me! I can laugh about it now

Jail

Turning myself in on a Friday was a big mistake. The regular processing folks were unavailable and I could not receive a jail house phone code or laundry services. However, God moved miraculously the minute I entered through the gates of that jail. Out of approximately 1,500 inmates, I was housed in the medical unit – because of my neck injury – with Matt Schiedel. I have known Matt since 7th grade. I was a youth pastor to his kids – Abbey, Doc, Julie and Lucy. Matt has since passed away but he was a great guy and a loyal friend. When I entered the medical unit, Matt's eyes almost popped out of his head. He was in a wheelchair at the time; he was in an accident while running from the police. The police beat him unconscious when they finally caught him. Matt taught me how to make coffee in jail. A blessing and half for an ex-cop who at one time drank 18 cups a day! He even lent me a clean pair of underwear when I had none. On my second day in jail one of the inmates in our unit cut an article out of the newspaper about me and circled my name in red. Someone took the article and left it on my bed in my cell. Matt (I'm very happy to report) watched my back the whole time and stood up for me on several occasions. My first experience on that side of bars was made so much easier due to Matt Schiedel. On Easter Sunday morning 1998, Matt and I put together an Easter Sunday service at 8:00 a.m., attended by 14 men. This by itself was a small miracle as Sunday mornings were normally the day every inmate sleeps late.

During this service, the "CERT" (Corrections Emergency Response Team) almost ended up lobbing tear gas at us. Our guard on duty in the medical unit knew we were having devotions and I can only assume this woman was the Devil. She got on the loudspeaker several times and told us we could not congregate together and we needed to disperse immediately. She then ordered us back to our cells but Matt decided to continue his preaching – as the CERT team gathered in full riot gear ready to pounce on us. I started praying like crazy because I most certainly did not want to get whacked with a nightstick or maced with pepper spray. No sooner did I stop praying when a corporal Matt and I had befriended walked up to our group and started hearing Matt preaching the Gospel. That corporal dismissed the CERT team and severally reprimanded the "devil guard" for pushing the riot alarm. This all took place while I was still in backsliding mode. Nine of those men prayed a prayer of salvation, including one flaming homosexual who stated, "Man, you guys must be telling the truth, look how hard the devil is working to stop you!"

I have to chuckle when judgmental people try and pass off jail time as some vacation resort with hot tubs and cable TV. I've spoken at enough prisons – and obviously my own experience gives me a degree of authority – to say they are hell holes. Maybe Martha Stewart had it "easy" but I don't really think she herself would say that.

While I was on the medical unit, I witnessed first-hand an 83-year old man – convicted of killing his wife – in dementia and he could only wear a diaper. I was beyond amazed how this poor guy was made to lie in his own filth because the nursing staff changed his diaper only once a day. Then there was a young black man who was obviously mentally deranged and belonged in a mental institution. He and I got into a short fight once because he was as unpredictable as he was volatile. I witnessed him placed in 'four point restraints' – this is where the guards chain you down to your bed by your hands and feet. This poor kid was made to lie in his own waste for three solid days. The stench of the medical ward became so bad at one point, all the nurses coming in the front entrance either gagged or covered their faces with a rag or a mask of some sort. We got used to it and never smelled a thing!

For some reason, there was no hot water in the medical ward. After not bathing for many days, I remember kneeling in the shower and filling my cupped hands with water, hoping to warm the water enough to splash it on a part of my body and then repeat the process. In this way I could at least feign some sort of bathing. After about three weeks in this unit, I was transferred to protective custody. This is (unfortunately) where they keep the juveniles who have been adjudicated as adults – as well as rapists, homosexuals, and … former police officers. It was actually Matt's idea that I ask to be placed in protection because I was an ex-cop. I only agreed to Matt's insistence for protection because at that time I figured Matt was closer to God than I was. I figured I can't be stupid (with my foolish pride) for the rest of my life. Again in the back of my warped mind, I figured if I got stabbed or if I hurt someone myself, I would scream to the newspapers about how wrongfully I thought I was being treated. How dumb, but that was my logic and thinking at the time!

There were many blessings in jail as well; I will only share a few with you. By this time my oldest daughter Mindy was graduating from high school. I was scheduled to be in jail for her high school graduation. I did start praying by then but my heart was devoid of any joy and it was more mechanical than anything else. I filled out a request to see my case worker; what a joke that was. When I told my case worker I wanted to apply for a day pass he almost fell out of his chair, laughing. He told me that in 20 years of working at the prison he had only seen two inmates get out on passes. One inmate received a pass when his child had brain surgery and the other went to a person whose mother had died. He also said those two guys got out in handcuffs and leg irons. He then asked me if I was stupid enough to embarrass my daughter like that. He said there was no chance of me getting out and that I should 'forgetaboutit.' I asked for the paperwork anyway and I arrogantly told God He should let me get out – for Mindy's sake. I knew in the back of my mind that I was going to use God's refusal to answer my prayer as an excuse to become even more bitter and angry when He did not let me out. I filled out the paperwork and for some reason, I prayed before I submitted it. While praying, out of the blue, my first attorney, Wallace "Skip" Bateman, popped into my mind like a thunderbolt. I had always regretted "firing" Skip from my initial case just because I found a "hot shot" Philadelphia lawyer who told me everything I wanted to hear. My lawyer (the one that was no good) even used the phrase "slam dunk" when it came to me being found not guilty – ha, lawyers.

Skip is not just a man of integrity, but has a good heart and is a great lawyer. Deborah called him for me and he went to work on the judge to plead for the day pass. I spoke to Skip one time while in jail and told him that if it were a matter of me getting out in chains, he should just drop it – I could not do that to Mindy. Skip Bateman got the day pass for me – no chains, no guards! Wow! I have always believed and taught my children that when God does something special for us and blesses us, He seems to always do it in a way that lets people say it was purely a coincidence. However, those of you who are familiar with how God works don't believe there are any coincidences when it comes to His work. It seems the more we testify to His goodness and the more we give God the credit for the wonderful things He does, the more wonderful things He does for us! The cycle continues as we give Him more glory, more praise, more of the "credit."

From some of the looks I received, I'm sure there were many "Christians" at Mindy's graduation who were annoyed at my presence there but I did not care. It was a Christian school and I figured their hypocrisy was on their own heads. There most certainly were some folks that were exceptionally kind to me and my family. I guess we have to learn to take the good with the bad? When Mindy's name was called and she received her diploma, she went out of her way to come down the aisle and hug her mother and me; she was not ashamed and it was one of the happiest moments of my life. I was starting to change!

I found out later that the guards who processed me and released me on my day pass purposely failed to tell me the ground rules. Specifically, I was not allowed to consume alcohol of any kind. They were hoping or perhaps assuming that I would be drinking while enjoying my temporary freedom. Their plan was that when I returned, they would give me a urine test and when I failed the test, I would (at the very least) lose my 16 days off for good behavior. I was so happy to be reunited with my kids and Deborah, drinking booze was the last thing on my mind and I did not lose my 16 days.

I had many other encounters with sadistic guards but probably the most heinous act I witnessed was not done to me. Another inmate who really had seen the error of his ways looked forward to seeing his wife and children every Tuesday. Week in and week out, I watched this man constantly avoid trouble as guard after guard did everything in his power to make the inmate's life miserable and provoke him. Our prayer and Bible study really seemed to keep him calm. On one particular Tuesday, one of the most evil guards in the unit lied to this man's wife, telling her that he was only allowed one visit per week and that his "girlfriend" had already been in to see him and that she (his wife) would have to leave. I can't imagine how heart broken that woman was, and we were all sad because we could not go tell her it was a damnable lie.

While in protective custody several of the inmates called me "Bible-man." One morning I was complaining about the grotesque powdered eggs we were being served and how I did not think even powdered eggs were supposed to have green stuff in them. Anyway, I made the comment out loud that they (the prison) should give us bacon – then we would have "green eggs and ham" and of course we all had a good laugh. One inmate said that he had been there six months and not once had they ever served bacon and another inmate said to me "why don't you pray for bacon-Aiken" – a little joke about my name I had not heard since I was about six. Anyway, I said "maybe I will." No, I didn't pray, but at breakfast three days later, we all received three strips of bacon. Actually it was more like cardboard with bacon flavor but the guys were so freaked out about this almost everyone on my block gave me one of his pieces of "bacon." Little miracles like that and my day pass happened to me all the time in jail.

So, apart from helping an innocent man (a Christian) get out of jail after being detained illegally just because he was from Columbia and wrongfully "labeled" a drug dealer, I taught two other men how to read; I read, I studied; I worked out. I was determined not to let jail beat me, and it didn't. On Day 74 I was discharged; What should have been a joyous time for a new beginning, with the exception of being re-united with my family, turned out to be anything but joyous. I don't think I would be here today if the Lord had not eventually rescued me, carried me back to safety, back to healing!

Getting out of jail was not as good as you might think.

After getting out of jail, I could not get a decent job to save my life. One "Christian" man threw my application back at me and said, "You've got to be kidding?" No matter how hard I tried, I could not seem to find decent employment anywhere. I did receive advice from the few friends that we had – they told me I should "move." But why? I knew I had not broken the law nor did I do the things I was accused of.; I dug in my heels and would not even consider re-locating. It wasn't long before I fell right back to my anger, bitterness, and defiance against God. As I said, I ran to the sport of racquetball. Some men have told me they went to tennis, fishing, weight lifting, or jogging. Some will go back to drugs or acting out sexually. When you are "off-balance" with God, in an effort to regain your balance, you will grab a-hold of the "familiar". You will revert to what you know as way of seeking the comfort you desire. When you lean too much on whatever it is that you grabbed on to, when you put too much of your weight into or on that "thing," you will fall right back into the trap that got you in trouble in the first place.   Many of us run to physically challenging sports to try to fill the void created by a lack of God's real presence in our lives. The problem people have in most modern churches is that they think they need to cover for God. Unable or unwilling to admit that something is wrong in their lives, people often end up "fronting" at church, pretending things are good on the outside, all while the inside is hurt, bruised, or damaged. Some run to drugs, sex, or any number of things to fill up time and emotional space. I sure did my fair share of all of the above, but I mainly ran to racquetball as my escape. Barb Moyer and I played together as mixed doubles partners for nearly five years. She and I – or I should say she – were so good, we were able to beat most men's doubles teams in our class. My father was actually her eighth grade science teacher. Playing with Barb was the one stabilizing force in my life at the time. However, God had other plans.

While making it to the finals in a doubles racquetball tournament with Barb, I dove for a ball, landing on my right shoulder and severely injuring it. With my right arm fully extended, I landed so hard, the force of my shoulder actually hurt my jaw. After a brief time out during this championship event, I decided to continue. My range of motion was less than thirty-five percent after the fall. I could not lift my right arm above my waist. I could not cock my arm for a strong forehand shot; I could only swing my hips around and hope that my arm would follow through with enough whip to make contact with the ball and at least get it back to the front wall. All of this effort and determination for a club championship, "ridiculous" is the only word that comes to mind now! After a complete month of rest, my shoulder showed little sign of improvement and I knew I needed a doctor. I could not reach for silverware, lift a cup of coffee, or any other ordinary task a right handed individual does every day. I remember holding my right arm up with my left hand in order to shave. Unfortunately, I went back to pain pills, drugs, and alcohol at that time. The MRI confirmed Dr. Spellman's diagnosis. I had landed so hard on my shoulder by diving on the hard floor, I tore my rotator cuff in three separate places. Any one tear, I was told, could be causing me the intense pain I felt. All three tears needed to be surgically repaired. The thought of that particular shoulder surgery was enough to turn my stomach. In those days they could not repair my shoulder orthoscopically; the technology now exists but was rare back then. A date for surgery was set. With no promise of a "recovery" sufficient enough to play racquetball at the same level, I fell into a major depression. Once again, I found the opportunity to blame God for my misfortune. It seemed like my life was over as I knew it. I continued to work as a bodyguard but the date for the surgery was hovering closer. Thank God my insurance company made me seek a second opinion. I had heard some good things from other racquetball players about Dr. Hurley in Sellersville, Pennsylvania, and I made an appointment outside my health network a month in advance. This forced me to postpone my original surgery date. Dr. Hurley looked at the films. He caused me more pain than the original injury but ended up asking me the $64,000 question: have you tried physical rehabilitation???? "An injury this serious? You gotta be kidding?" I was never a believer in rehab but, to make a long story short, in four months I was playing again, and in nine months I was finally once again competing at the level where I had been. That's the fun part.........

In professional sports such as golf, tennis, rugby, racquetball, we all have one thing in common: a lot of us will never be heard of by the general public. We play with the big boys but there is not much celebrity status in those sports per se. We do it for the love of the game – the money is secondary. I probably earned a hundred dollars one year. Even volleyball does not pay well unless you are the best of the best. You get the picture. I spent almost nine months with the most wonderful rehab specialist named Wendy Detwieler. She literally worked me back to playing form, I still owe her a big chocolate bar for the phenomenal job she did rehabilitating my shoulder. Now if I could just get my soul rehabilitated!

Chapter 6
WHEN WILL I LEARN?

It's sad when true brothers and sisters in Christ do not and may never agree; the Devil thrives on our "divisions." Having said that, I do think there are times division is necessary, just like in the Bible when tribes that moved together did not get along. The tribal leaders would often agree to split for the betterment of both tribes. Here's where we as Christians miss it. Those tribal leaders – "real men" – knew this was dangerous. They often wept together because they knew how dangerous it was to lose half of their protection. Oh yes, make no mistake about it, this "split" would cost each of them dearly in protection from future enemies.

Moving up to modern military times… In the military, when out on patrol, it's customary for a platoon of men to send out a "point man." The point man is the person who goes a fair distance ahead of the platoon and is often the one wounded or killed first. He is supposed to check in at regular intervals. Prior to being falsely accused, I ran "point" – out there actually doing many "good deeds." We were feeding the hungry through our ministry. We were getting kids off the streets and we were really making a difference until I lost my moorings with God. When was the last time I attended a church service? I mean, checked in with headquarters? You understand what I'm saying here; I strayed way off course. Metaphorically, I was out in the jungle. Every time someone called me on the radio and asked how I was doing, I told them I was "all right." Was I fooling myself? You bet! Pride is the biggest self-deceiver of all. The very nature of pride is that the person who has it never knows how badly he is infected. Just like modern day soldiers send out scouts and continue an ancient practice that dates back to Biblical times, I was out there all right, out there doing my own thing, thinking I was "all that" because I ran a street ministry. I reassured myself that I knew this "jungle" like the back of my hand and I was perfectly safe. My success, my seniority, or a combination of both fooled me into thinking they (other Pastors) did not know what they were talking about. I was the "expert." Expert? – more like an idiot.

In March of 2000, Barry, as he had done while I was in jail, went to the food market where Deborah worked and tried one last time to convince my wife to leave me and that he would "take care of her" – this was all caught on the stores video tape. This particular day, knowing that I was finally off probation, I drove to Barry's house like a madman. I had every intention of beating him or die trying, even though I knew it would probably land me back in jail. Keep in mind, Barry is about 6'2 or 6'3 and outweighed me by about 80 to 100 lbs. Even though I knew I would be arrested, I remember saying in the car – "Sorry God, you said no more than we can handle and I've had it with this *expletive deleted*! Do something, cause I'm gonna." Don't you love it when God's patience with us is so much deeper than anyone could ever imagine on this side of eternity? I squealed into Barry's driveway just as Judy *(not her real name)* got out of the car in their very long driveway. I did not see Barry so I stopped the car at the edge of the driveway near the road and got out. I never left the side of my car and the closest I ever got to Judy and her kids was about 30 yards away. With my exceptionally loud voice, I knew I was close enough to her that she would hear me clearly and she did. Choosing my words carefully, I got out my car and yelled: "Tell that piece of s*#t husband of yours to stay away from my wife, or <u>he WILL</u> suffer the consequences!"

Judy did not say a word but just looked at me in shock as if I had three heads. With that, and knowing she would be calling the police, I left.

Of course, I received the obligatory summons in the mail. I have no doubt that had I been on probation at the time it would have meant: *go directly to jail, do not pass go, do not collect 200 dollars.* With zero money for groceries, my house in foreclosure, and our electric about to be shut off again, I phoned Skip Bateman and told him I sure could not afford a lawyer. Skip was great (again) and got the charges dropped.

Although nobody in his right mind would say that everything bad that happens to someone is a direct result of their failure or sin, I have no doubt that this "arrest" was in direct proportion to my relapse into anger, bitterness, drug and alcohol use. This particular arrest was the two by four applied to my thick skull that finally made me realize I was heading in the wrong direction, again! Thank you, Lord, and yes, yes, I FINALLY learned my lesson. I became a new man and it's been that way for almost twelve years (as I write this). Barry may be facing his own hell on earth but I can't be concerned about that. As I said, I actually pray for Barry and Harriet's mother, Joan, from time to time.

God Wants Us to Put This Time to Good Use

You may recall the story in John Chapter 9 when the disciples asked Jesus why a particular man was born blind. The crowd took the very normal assumption that either he or his parents sinned and this is why he was blind. Jesus answered the mystery for us when he said: *"Neither this man .... but so the glory of God could be revealed."*

So it does happen. Subsequently there are times when God does cause great fish to swallow people up. When we refuse to acknowledge sin in our lives, God is so incredibly patient with us – He warns us, begs us … I'm convinced that we human beings must actually fight with God for Him not to get our attention. When and if we are ever foolish enough to do that, HE CAUSES the fish to swallow us. The truth is, if you're not growing closer to the Lord, you are either going backwards, or you have become too comfortable. When you get comfortable with your Christianity is when you settle for a certain amount of "tolerable sin." There really is no such thing, but we like to fool ourselves into believing that there is. When you're in the belly of a fish – take it from me, I've been there – you have two choices: continue to do it your way and become bitter, cold-hearted, and hard; or, begin to allow the Lord to work things out in your life, surrender to Him and allow Him to pick up the pieces.

But if God is real how can he let so much bad stuff happen?

What kind of God would allow little children to be killed and allow the world to be filled with so much hate?

These two questions or variations of them have been asked by mankind – probably since Adam and Eve's day. Of course Adam and Eve knew first-hand the answer to those questions for it is because of them that evil entered into the world. Now before you jump the gun too quickly and blame them for all that is wrong in the world today, I have always believed that even though Adam and Eve were the first two human beings, they, like so many Biblical figures after them, represent a type of us. That is not to say I do not believe these people really didn't exist – I think they did. But they – Job, Moses, Adam, Sampson, Delilah –

all lived lives as examples for you and me. It's easy to ignore the God of the Bible because so much evil exists in the world today. So much of life seems unfair, unkind, and hateful, but this was never God's intention for us. When we choose to sin against God, our sins are the purest form of rebellion against the One God who created us, who intended us to live in fellowship with Him through all eternity but – because we have fallen under our own sins – our sentence is death!

However, there is GOOD NEWS!

The good news is that the same God who created you loves you so much He could not stand to see you separated from His Love, His Goodness, His desire for you to live forever with Him in a place called Heaven!

I heard a Mennonite preacher tell a story once – it went something like this. He and his family were at the beach one day and while he was watching his baby daughter, he ran into someone he knew. His wife and other children were swimming. The preacher started a conversation with this acquaintance and his two or three year old daughter began to dig in the sand. Speaking to this friend for just a minute or two, he looked down at his daughter and to his shock she was gone! While frantically looking around and not seeing her, he later said that he could have been talking to the president of the United States or another important world figure, but at that moment it would not have meant a darn thing to him – HIS DAUGHTER WAS MISSING! I don't know too many parents who have not had that gut-wrenching, stomach falling, sinking feeling at one time or another with regards to their own children. Fortunately in this pastor's story, his little girl had only wandered a few yards away and the view of her was obstructed by the throngs of bathers walking up and down the beach.

Now take that gut-wrenching, missing child feeling and realize that is how the God who created you feels about YOU! He never intended for us to have to live through all this misery, he never intended for us to have to feel the heart ripping pain of death and separation – so He made a way! He sent His son, His ONLY son, down here a little over two thousand years ago to die just for you. In this way, after you breath your last, it is then and only then that you will be reunited with your Creator. Think about it. Even atheist scientists believe a man named Jesus lived two thousand plus years ago. They may not agree about who he was or what he was doing here, but they are never foolish enough to deny he existed. Yes, in case you have not caught on yet, Jesus Christ sacrificed his sinless life so that the penalty for our sins would be paid in full. In the Old Testament and throughout ancient civilizations, men have always made sacrifices to their gods. Jesus, who knew no sin, freely gave up his life for us. It is the only sacrifice a holy and just God could accept to pay the eternal price of mankind's continual disobedience. Then, to prove that Jesus really was who He claimed to be, on the third day – unlike Houdini or anybody else – He rose from the dead to never die again.

Does God or Satan make bad things happen?

How could Satan have the freedom to do these terrible things to godly people? Unfortunately, Satan has a legal claim to attack and influence us, using our own free will against us. Sometimes he gets "license" because of our sins and sometimes he can attack when we are counting on things other than Christ's
shed blood on the Cross.

No, you don't have to dig around constantly searching and searching – God is more than capable of bringing thoughts to your mind of situations that are not in line with His will. Although this "spiritual checklist" needs to be maintained our entire time down here on earth, we do get rest and plenty of it. It should eventually come to a point where the Devil can't look at us and smirk and impose his harassment on us any more. Never forget that your righteousness is what "filthy rags" are to God…. I prefer to look at myself as a piece of debris; it's biblical and it just makes things easier that way. According to my understanding of scripture, IF you are a Christian, this was allowed to happen to you because you were off course – somehow, Satan had a legal claim to do this thing to you.

OUR CONVERSION EXPERIENCE

Back in 1981 after three years of earnestly searching for answers to life's questions, my drinking had become habitual. If I were an alcoholic, I guess I would have been considered a "working" one because with few exceptions, I never missed work or messed up due to my drinking. My temper and my anger – now that's a different story. Although not yet married by then Deborah, Mindy, and I, were living together as a "family." I was prone to a lot of screaming, hollering, and breaking things. A few times the police came to our apartment; they were usually friends of mine and would simply warn me to "keep it down." One time Deborah was trying to have me arrested and a police sergeant smirked at her and said, "Yeah right, lady." I'm not proud of any of this reprehensible behavior, but it was how we lived until Deborah packed up and left me, moving back to New Jersey while I stayed in Pennsylvania. I was about 26 years old and continued drinking heavily and "enjoying" my re-found "bachelor-life." I remember waking up one morning and having to kick empty beer bottles around by my bed just to find some empty floor space. Mindy had looked to me as her father and I started to miss her and Deborah and I actually started feeling guilty (something I had not felt much while growing up). Deborah and I continued to talk on the phone as couples often do – *should we break up? should we get married? I love you, I hate you,* just a typical mixed up young couple with no direction. When we were living together, Deborah and I often watched television Evangelist Jimmy Swaggart, the same preacher I mentioned earlier and for whom I later did some volunteer work. We would watch Swaggart on TV as a combination of penance and comedy. I remember saying to Deborah once, "Is this a great country or what? Where else can you go to church in your living room and drink beer at the same time?" One time Swaggart stopped his preaching and pointed at the television screen and said; "I see you there swigging your beer sir!" I was in mid swig and an eruption of beer left my mouth and nose, making a mess of me and the chair in which I was seated. With Deborah moving back to New Jersey and living with her father, I had seen on TV that Jimmy Swaggart was appearing at the civic center in Philadelphia. I called an old girlfriend and took her to see him with me. We I did not stay long and for whatever reason, I did not take her to my home that night, choosing rather to drop her off at her place. About one o'clock in the morning that night, while channel surfing, I stumbled across Jimmy Swaggart on TV. I decided to watch, thinking it was a replay of the service I had attended just hours earlier. It wasn't, but Rev. Swaggart preached a simple message about how God can change your life if you let him, and boy <u>did my life need changing!</u> Swaggart told the listening audience to pray a simple prayer with him and I decided I had nothing to lose, so I prayed. I prayed and I bawled my eyes out, feeling so bad about all the lies I had told in my life and for the way I treated Deborah (the nicest person I had ever met). Later I fell sound asleep without my customary routine of drinking myself to sleep. The next morning Deborah and I were on the phone and I said to her, "You're never gonna believe what I did last night." She replied, "You're never going to believe what I did last night!" She told me how she went to the Chestnut Assembly of God church in Vineland, New Jersey. She said that she prayed with Pastor Ralph Snook to give her heart to Christ. This was done on the exact same night that I had prayed; only we were in two different states and did not even know the other was even going to church. You may say that is a coincidence, but I call it a minor miracle from God. Deborah and I have been together ever since. Next to salvation, Deborah is the best gift God ever gave me.

Chestnut Assembly of God church, Vineland New Jersey

If you find yourself in a terrible situation and you have never known what it is to be Born Again, this thing happened to you because you need to get re-united with your Creator. Satan was allowed to ruin you because you gave him license. Somewhere, somehow, he had a legal claim to do that to you. Keep in mind he (the Devil) wants to ruin you still.

I think we all have that specific part of human nature that wants to shift blame for what may be happening to us: my wife left me for another man, my husband drinks too much, my son tells me he is a homosexual! The reality is that NOTHING can happen to you as a child of God unless God first allows this happen **Romans 8:28**. This is a tough thing to say to people that suffered through the 9-11 World Trade Center and Pentagon bombings, the recent earthquake and subsequent tsunami in Indonesia, Hurricane Katrina, or any number of disasters that befall us.

Often I have heard scripture slightly quoted out of context: ...***Remember God would not allow you to go through anything HE knows you can't handle.***

Comforting, maybe? Scriptural, not exactly. It's true according to I Corinthians 10:13; God will not allow us to be tempted above that which we are able to stand AND with every temptation HE makes a way of escape. When tough times hit your life, HE does not allow it to be so "God-awful" that you must turn to sin to relieve yourself of the pain. This brings us back to our main point. WHATEVER it is that is gripping your life today, know that God allowed it to happen and HE will bring good out of it sooner or later **if you allow Him to**! Notice I did not say He MADE it happen; often this is not the case. Is God trying to get your attention? Whatever it is you're going through, I promise that you will be a stronger and a better person when it is over, IF you acquiesce to His calling.

Chapter 7
YOU ARE NOT ALONE

I am becoming increasingly more concerned and alarmed for our country as more and more police and wanna-be district attorneys seem more concerned with gaining convictions than they are at getting to the truth. The famous "Duke Lacrosse case" was a perfect example of this. Maybe I was the same way when I was a cop? What goes around does come around. **Galatians 6:7** In his book, *No Retreat, No surrender*, Tom Delay does an excellent job of describing these exact same tactics used by Democrats on a national level.

Along those same lines, I am starting to witness the same prosecutorial fanaticism in southern Arizona. This time it is aimed at good people who are doing their best to keep illegal immigrants from entering this country illegally. The most outspoken are being charged with trumped up charges even when these individuals are on their own property! Good men who want only the best for our country are being charged and made into criminals. The famous Mexican flag burner, Roy Warden could write an entire book about how those in public office, routinely break the rule of law in their on-going effort to silence him. It's beyond critical down here, and government officials now seem to be going after Federal Border Agents on trumped up charges in similar fashion, but this will have to be a topic for another book.

It's during your dark and gloomy times, when we are waiting on the Lord, that I think we get the most anxious. I have talked to many Christian men who have been fired or lost their jobs, sometimes through no fault of their own, only to take a job that in a million years you would never expect them to be doing. For instance, one of my best friends went from being an airline pilot and flying nationwide, to being an electrical laborer. The uncertainty of the future and perhaps the unhappiness of the present often make us cry out (or complain) to God. I'm sure my friend cried out to God many times: **"WHY?"** I'm equally sure God answered his prayer in one of three ways – **yes**, **no**, or **wait**. In his case, as with many, the answer was "wait." This same friend is now a pilot again working for the FAA. For those of us that take our Christianity seriously, there is a growth process, and sometimes that process can be painful. During periods when the answer is "wait," FAITH is required the most. The term "waiting on the Lord" really has at it's core meaning, praying! Often these are the times when we either are not hearing from God or are not listening. These are times that can get so awful for us, try our patience, challenge our core beliefs and our FAITH, but as the Bible says, "… without faith it is impossible to please God." **Hebrews 11:6** These are the times when we can become the most anxious, the most bitter, and the most rebellious. **These are the times when we make choices, fall back into an old sin habit, or trust God and keep praying!**

We can listen to sermons all day long about how "God is in control" and often times we want to scream, "So why isn't God listening to me?" I have been there and I know myself that I often feel embarrassed because God truly does work it out for those who simply put their trust in Him. Nobody said it was easy – if it were easy everybody would do it – but it is real to us and not some pie in the sky, utopian, feel good philosophy!

As I said, sometimes God's answer is, "No." When that happens, I promise you will be the first to know it. In the meantime, wait. Believe it or not, waiting patiently often is a part of the growth process.

Looking back on my "hay-days" of running YouthQuest I can see I simply failed to rely on God anymore. I got to the point, because of the many blessings I was receiving, of believing that everything I did WAS God's will. Although I knew and taught all the right things, my actions behind the scenes were the exact opposite. Outbursts of anger at home, a controlling and domineering attitude towards my wife and children would eventually sentence me to God's "breaking process." I had no prayer life to speak of and my Bible reading was almost non-existent. If any of my Christian brothers or sisters saw this pride in me, they never said anything.

I don't think learning the life of a surrendered Christian comes from reading books (except the Bible) or from teachers. In the book of Galatians it talks about; "Falling from Grace". I no longer believe that this means truly converted, born again Christian, can lose their salvation. But rather, that he or she is looking towards something other than faith in Jesus and what He did for you personally on the Cross. That's God's grace you can fall from. There are certain things that you are going to want to do to help solidify and make permanent your return to the Lord. Going to church, reading your Bible, praying. You may be amazed by what you discover. When we don't submit to God's authority, His training in our lives, we eventually fall because *we got off course*! Think about it, it is no more complicated than that. I got off course. I was on a pathway to death, both physical and spiritual.

Sin IS a Dirty Word

Most sins are pleasurable, temporarily. We all carry our own personal sins. There really is no new sin since the bible was written, but rather modern day sins are only derivatives of those of old. As I speak to men's groups I often ask the audience – if I had a syringe filled with all the pleasures the world has to offer and I could inject you with it, bringing you pleasure, happiness, fulfillment, and everything that would allow all of your earthly dreams to come true, would you let me inject it into your body? Now before you answer that, there is only one catch. This same syringe contains one living cancer cell in it or H.I.V. or Ebola. Would anyone in the audience allow me to inject him knowing the risk that the cancer cell may divide and start growing?

Surprisingly, that is exactly what many of us do; I know I have. I exchanged my future, my well being, for the excitement of a temporary fix. We accept the fleeting pleasures of the moment with the cancer cell in return for the pleasure we get from our "secret sin." Probably the number one problem men in churches tell me they have is with Internet pornography! In 2007 it was reported that there is more FREE internet pornography available than all the internet porn combined back in 1999. In the privacy of their own homes, men seek the fix of the high that comes from this "cancer" and never bother to question the harm they do to themselves and their families when they indulge. Today addictions are rampant in Christian churches. We have lost our way because under the guise of not wanting to offend anyone our pulpits are silent!

This is exactly what happens when it "appears" we are getting away with whatever it is we do in secret. The Bible is very clear: sin leads to death. **Romans 6:23** It may not be immediate, and the death that is promised may not be that of a loved one or even your own… but death will occur. It may be as profound as the death of an unborn baby because of the sin of adultery or fornication. Or, it can be more subtle like the death of a marriage or relationship, or the loss of a job or finances. There is no mistaking it, it has been decreed by God Himself – **the wages of sin is death!** For so many men these days and now, more and more women, pornography becomes their secret, personal sin. In American society, we are buried over our heads in the sin of lust – from soft porn Victoria's Secret catalogs to Britney Spears slithering in a sexual manner on stage in front of millions of 10 and 11 year olds. Our entire moral system does not have far to go before it actually does bottom out, as demonstrated so many times throughout world history. This will eventually result in attacks on Christianity and Christians unlike anything we have ever seen in our lives. These attacks already started with crucifixes in jars of urine called "art" and other "art" exhibits such as the "Christ Killa" at the Niche LA Video Art gallery in Los Angeles. An exhibit that invited participants to shoot hordes of "homicidal Jesus Christs." You won't see any "art" like that involving Mohammed any time soon! This blatant disrespect for Christianity is only a precursor of what will come as actual violence against Christians. So much for the "tolerance" promoted by the left.

It is already starting to happen. When a young valedictorian can have her microphone cut off by school officials because she chooses to thank her God for her success, how far can we be from making evangelism illegal in this country? Ann Coulter wrote an extraordinary book about this called *Godless, the Church of Liberalism*. (As an aside, I had Ann on my radio show a few times and she was the last guest of the last show I did on KVOI in Tucson.)

Attacks and arrests of Christian home schooling families are starting to take place at an unprecedented rate. With the help of the National Education system, MTV and others that hold an inordinate amount of sway with our children, they have created a whole generation of children who are no longer capable of using their imaginations or being creative. As a whole, children today spend more time piercing themselves, cutting and burning themselves, and getting tattoos then they do writing songs or poetry. Even the very music they listen to must be accompanied by visual effects or music videos. I-Pods, Nano-pods, CD's, Multi-media devices. It's no longer good enough to simply hear a song on the radio, kids today must have that visual experience as well. We are dumb-ing our kids down faster than we realize! Children today cannot grasp concepts, thoughts, and ideas like they once did. This plays into the hands of the foundations of liberalism/socialism in this country because liberalism is based on emotion and feeling rather than reason and logic.

In many European countries the amount of sexual content on TV has served to numb the senses of exposed children. The same thing is starting to happen in the U.S. The dumber the kids, the less likely they are to challenge what they are taught in some of our dreadful public schools. By raising an entire generation of spineless, dependant children. The greatest country the world has ever known will soon be a thing of the past. We are losing by default!

Take for instance Israel

Keep not thou silence, O God: hold not thy peace, and be not still, O God. For, lo, thine enemies make a tumult: and they that hate thee have lifted up the head. They have taken crafty counsel against thy people, and consulted against thy hidden ones. They have said, Come, and let us cut them off from being a nation; that the name of Israel may be no more in remembrance. **Psalm 83:1-4**

What in the world could the nation of Israel have to do with the dumb-ing down of our children? I often said on my radio show that the barometer of the world is the Nation of Israel. After about a 2000 year prophetic drought, Israel becoming a nation again in 1948 was the "super-sign" of Bible prophecy being fulfilled! From everything I have read all future prophecy in the Bible is in some way connected to Israel. These prophecies concerning, Iraq, Iran, one world government, the mark of the Beast, are now starting to take place right before our very eyes. I don't think it is a coincidence that anti-Israeli sentiment continues to grow in the United States. That tiny little nation about the size of New Jersey is still at the center of God's will in the earth. It has been fought over for thousands of years and is still being fought over today.

I also believe that the enemies of Israel will one day attack Israel en masse from the north just as the book of Revelation predicts. Perhaps this will be done for heretfore undiscovered natural gas or oil under Israel. I won't be one bit surprised if Israel one day soon, goes at it alone and takes out the nuclear capabilities of Iran. This in and of itself might be reason enough for the world to attack! If I am reading my Bible correctly, when Israel is finally attacked by her enemies, it is then that five-sixths of Israel will be wiped out. Complete annihilation of Israel will only be stopped by the direct intervention of God Himself! The United States has given it's word that it will defend Israel under these conditions. I seriously doubt that we will. By then, our selfish, self-centered, American, MTV generation, will not be inclined to lift a finger to help. This is all part of God's plan, so not to worry!

MTV, like so many others, has learned the importance of early childhood indoctrination. Take for instances the Wahhabies of Saudi Arabia. For over 30 years radical Muslims, Palestinians, and Wahhabists from Saudi Arabia have been teaching their children that to hate and kill Jews and Christians is the ultimate service to their Muslim god. It's no wonder radical Muslims can say with confidence that thousands of homicide bombers and those willing to sacrifice their lives are pouring into society for the express purpose of taking over the world by force. The **modus operandi** of radical Islam is to; INFILTRATE, ASSIMILATE, then DOMINATE. For the most part our politicians are sitting on their hands with regard to this growing phenomenon! If you think "all politicians are bums," go find one you know who isn't. If you can't find one, then I guess that means you are the only person you can find who is not a bum and you should run for election yourself. Join the deacon board of your church or whatever your passion and calling is, follow it, pursue it, in other words – don't just sit there, get involved!

The Islamic influence in Europe is being seen now more clearly than just a few short years ago. Believe it or not, much of Europe's disapproval of the United States has its roots (spiritually speaking) in what used to be our modest restraint. What we are willing to show on TV or print has continued to spiral down morally. The entire snobbish, condescending attitude towards us held by the French, Canadians, and many Europeans has its spiritual roots in their view of Americans as prudes. No "high society," social elite ever wants to be known as "prudish." This is why many European countries are starting to experience the backlash of dormant radical Islam. The same will start to happen in the U.S. soon.

To the Left, being a Christian or even a Republican means no fun, very boring, and no sex. This is why the socialist left – the "progressives" – are determined to pull down every barrier of decent behavior in society. Sexual degeneration of every imaginable kind exists in this country now. The United States has become Sodom and Gomorrah light! Perversion of children is so rampant on the Internet and in many major cities in the U.S., it is no wonder that many men in Christian churches are addicted to some form of pornography or another. The world has influenced the church more than many of us are willing to admit, it is supposed to be the other way around! When you couple this with the environment of death we have created in society through abortion and the casual way we regard life, you find that the churches today are ill-equipped to help those in need, they have been neutered. Just this one sin of pornography alone, has crippled many otherwise outstanding men and has had an untold, detrimental effect on our country, it's staggering! The **addiction factor**, the **adrenaline rush,** that comes from these things are as powerful on the brain as the strongest narcotic.

WHEN OBSESSION OVERTAKES REASON

Not long ago, NBC ran a series about "online predators" where grown men, thinking they were chatting online with under-age children, lined up one after another to meet these "children" for sex. District attorneys, Rabbi's, Police Officers, NBC filmed dozens of men as they were led away in handcuffs through this way overdue, and much needed, sting operation.

It is the exact same "adrenaline rush" people get when they are having an affair and think they are in "love." We play with a loaded pistol when we enter into such relations forbidden by God. These emotions, fueled by adrenaline and the release of dopamine in our brains are strong enough to pull down Christian leaders, or anybody for that matter. This is why God warns us in the Bible to, STAY AWAY, FLEE, RUN, and don't look back! How much trouble could I have saved myself if I just would have taken my own advice all those years ago?

One person's "personal demons" will not necessarily be the same as someone else. Remember, growing as a Christian is not about being good, it is about being better! In order to grow and mature, you must become a person who seeks "TRUTH" at all levels, regardless of how it may affect you. It is then that you are on your way to being "rescued."

It pains me that many Christians and churches refuse to hear or learn from mature Christians who have been through and seen much of what I speak of in this book. However, there is hope. My current Pastor, Bruce Brock of the Faith Community Church in Tucson Arizona is a classic example. Bruce is a man being used mightily by God in spite of his personal failures long ago. There are thousands, perhaps tens of thousands of former Pastor's and church leaders who have "fallen" for one reason or another. Most of them NEVER return to any position within Christian service. One reason is the large amount of Christians out there who have determined that they (the fallen) have forever forfeited their right to any kind of leadership. The idea that anyone can determine whether or not someone can return to Christian service is a wholly man-made doctrine, subjective, and not biblical. As I said earlier about Jimmy Swaggart, it's crucially wrong and contrary to Galatians chapter 6 verses 1and 2.

In praying for Pastor Bruce Brock of Tucson Arizona one day, I believe the Lord showed me why (in spite of his failings many, many, years ago) he and his ministry are so blessed by God today. Put simply, Bruce never forgot where he came from. ***He who has been forgiven much, loves much!*** I have met several Pastors who have returned to full time ministry but make the crucial mistake of trying to hide or cover their public sins of the past.

One Pastor Friend of mine in particular, has had the same church and the same amount of people for many years. Same amount of people, but completely different faces. Unfortunately, because he is not candid about his failings and his wife has never really been healed of the hurt inflicted by his actions so long ago, his church remains stagnant. He is however, a tremendous preacher, but when someone new comes along and mysteriously discovers his "past". They inevitably cause a split in his church and the cycle starts all over again. This has been going on for many years. Pastor Bruce of Tucson taught me amend this lesson in this regard. By refusing to try and hide his past, he constantly reminds his flock that neither he nor us are immune to sin. That, in my opinion is the difference! Certainly those who never learn, or are never willing to let go of the sin or sins that so beset them would not qualify for a leadership role. But there are many more that are currently disconnected from the Body who, given half a chance, would once again become great warriors for the cause of Christ. They have been sidelined by the enemy waiting for true believers to come and help restore them. **Gal. 6:1**

Christians who are nowhere to be found are often the ones who have been hurt the most in church. How much faster could many of us begin our "healing" if the church just took the time to restore those "fallen" to "fellowship." Sadly, the church as a whole is either unwilling or incapable of following its own Biblical mandate to RESTORE such a one in the spirit of meekness. Regardless, I'm convinced that as we grow in the faith and knowledge of God, HE does help us rid ourselves of sins for which we have a preponderance. I can't count the amount of times in my life that "STOP SIGNS" abounded. Unfortunately, when we run too many stop signs in life – be they spiritual or factual – one of two spiritual things will eventually happen: **a.** you'll either get pulled over and arrested; or **b.** you'll get into a crash! Boy, did I get into a few spiritual crashes before the Lord finally got a grip on some of my sinful habits. We always have a free choice – a free will – to obey God or not. IF you are seeking the TRUTH in all matters concerning your life, then all of us would begin to live and get along so much better. I'm not there yet, neither are you! But I have left my old life that ship has sailed! I can look behind and see I'm not what I was, and when I look forward I see I'm not yet what I will become. The thing about life that never ceases to amaze me about Christianity is that we never seem to stop learning. Well, some of us do, more on that in a minute. Every one of us, to some degree or another, is born with an instinct to know more, to learn more about life, or to figure things out. There is a hole, a void, at the core of all people's being. This is not new to many of you; for some however, it is the first time hearing this message.

Many people try to fill that void in their soul with various "things" that never seem to satisfy. Many movie stars claim they have found the secrets to the "meaning of life" – only these same false prophets refuse to have their views challenged in an open forum of any kind. They keep their "public forum" limited to arenas where they control not only the discussion but the environment as well.

Chapter 8
Progressives – Liberals;
a different religion!

I honestly believe that to be a liberal in this country today, you must reach a point where you simply stop learning and stop seeking truth. Contrary to popular belief, TRUTH is not subjective – it is absolute. This is why Jesus could (truthfully) call himself "…THE way, THE TRUTH, and THE life." He went on to say; nobody can get to God except through Him. **John 14:6**

In order to be a liberal today, not only do you have to stop learning, they reach a plateau where they think they have all the answers to life's problems and push an emotional agenda full of gobbledy goop on others as if they were the ultimate expert. To be a liberal today you must try to prove right is wrong and wrong is right. You must be committed to pulling down everything good and knowingly or unknowingly, you must be committed to failure and failed policies. To be a liberal today means the world will often bow at your feet, especially if you are from Hollywood or there is a PhD at the end of your name. Yes, liberals think they have all the answers to life's problems but in reality, they offer nothing but more problems as solutions to those problems. Among many of Liberalism's "contributions" to society so far have brought us the; highest tax rates in our nation's history, a failed welfare system, a social security system that will eventually fail, open southern borders, weak national defense, the *thought police*, the *food police*, the *smoke police*, the *speech police*, *light bulb police*, an attempt to resurrect the "fairness doctrine", and surrender in Iraq, just to name a few.

Let me give you just one small example of liberals in action:

For many years un-elected bureaucratic (liberal) eggheads spent much time and effort putting small farmers in the U.S. out of business. They did this in the name of environmental protection. In the 1990's small family farmers who grew corn or were dairy farmers simply could not keep up with mountainous regulations, so many of them just stopped. Either that, or when the family owned farm was passed to the next generation, that generation could not possibly pay the estate or capital gains taxes on the land and they were forced to sell. Either way, the results were the same, the government succeeded in putting them out of business.

Then we started to hear about the myth of "man-made" global warming, later changed to "climate change". A concerted effort by the government saw us leaning more and more towards ethanol products made from corn and other food sustenance and away from petroleum based products made from oil. Now, the very corn needed to produce ethanol is becoming more scarce. What does that do? It makes the price of corn go up. Those prices do not go up in a vacuum, they hit poor Latino countries who live on corn meal as well as us in the United States who drink milk or eat cereal. Where does the milk come from? It comes from cows, what do cows eat, CORN! Where do we get the corn and the cows? From farmers, many of the same farmers who have been forced out of business by our own government! Liberals and progressives are no good-do good-ers, who only offer short-term solutions to problems by creating more long-term problems.

Pat Buchanan was correct to talk about the "culture war" in this country.

A republic once equally poised must either preserve its virtue or lose its liberty.
John Witherspoon

Two times in my life Pat Buchanan made me cringe. He was right both times, just a little ahead of his time. The first time was when he and I were driving from Philadelphia to New York. At one point on I-95 there was a barrier about 70 feet high, the type built along major highways to block the noise from the highway to the adjoining neighborhoods. Mr. Buchanan pointed to the barrier and said, "See Steve, that is exactly what we need between us and Mexico." Although I said "yes, sir" as if I were in complete agreement with him, I remember thinking how over-the-top this was. Of course, only ten years later I ended up living near 'Terrorist Alley' in the heart of illegal immigration, human and drug trafficking: Tucson, Arizona. How right Pat Buchanan was.

Pat Buchannan

The other time Pat Buchanan made me cringe was when he began to talk about a "culture war." Much has

140

been written and said about the culture war raging in America today. As Pat Buchanan said, it is a "war" for the very heart and soul of the United States of America. Great social leaders of this country such as Pat Buchanan, Janet Parshal, Bev LaHaye, Tim LaHaye, and the likes of Phyllis Schlafly, Gary Bauer, Bill Bennett, D. James Kennedy, James Dobson, and many others have been talking about this "culture war" for some time. It is here NOW! Whether it is the promotion of abortion, or no fault divorce, prayer in school, removal of the Ten Commandments, homosexuality, gun control, public decency, or any number of other things, the "culture war" is in full swing! With 40 plus years of controlling the House and Senate, the Democrat Party got many "things" done. Unfortunately for us, many of the "things" were wrong for this country and headed us on the slippery slope towards debauchery and socialism. Margaret Thatcher once said; "the problem with socialism is that sooner or later, you run out of other people's money". All we need to do today is look at the tidal wave of illegal immigration into the country and our own government's refusal to take any real action to stop it. As we watch helplessly while those in power rush us into a multifarious North American Continent. We are watching our nation being given away, inch by inch, corporation by corporation, right under our noses.

At no time did the "power" of those who desire a globalist approach to American life – indeed open borders with Mexico and Canada – show itself to me than in September of 2006. That was when I witnessed first-hand "the powers that be" pull out all the stops in a lonely Congressional race in Arizona's Eighth Congressional District. (More on that later.)

Congressman and Presidential Candidate, Tom Tancredo and I in 2006.

Coupled with illegal immigration is the "holy grail" of the liberal Left – **abortion**! In 2001, before 9/11, Senator Charles Schumer of New York broke a long standing taboo of the Senate Judicial Committee. Senator Schumer held hearings, essentially making public what previously was known about only behind closed doors. The question asked was: should the ideology of a judicial nominee be considered in the judicial appointee process?

I attended several of those meetings. When Senator Schumer held those meetings, it was as if he was gaining support for what he knew had to be done – President Bush's nominees had to be stopped – especially when said "nominee" had the remotest chance of being nominated to the Supreme Court. Many of the discussions – behind the scenes of course – revolved around one issue: abortion. For whatever reason, the liberal Left has a death grip (pun intended) on the so-called right a woman has been given to kill her unborn baby. Personally, I don't get it. The Left could make so much more progress in this country if it would lose its stranglehold on the issue of abortion. Maybe there is divine intervention in all this; I suspect there is. For me the answer to the question of when life begins is easy. **Life begins when cells start to divide.** If that is not the beginning of life, then I do not know what is. Coupled with the fact that a baby growing inside its mother's womb, does not receive any blood from its mother. Nutrients in, waste out. This is how babies often have a different blood type then their mother, they are individuals.

Mrs. Virginia Evers-Inventor of the 10 week old feet pin.

The battle line in this aspect of the culture war became clear to us when Senator Schumer pulled off those hearings. 9-11 came not long after that and the good senator's work was put on the shelf. For the most part the Democrat Party wants nothing more than power.

Democrats run around trying to retrieve their power lost when Dick Gephardt handed over the gavel of the U.S. House of Representatives to Newt Gingrich. It was then that liberals started seething inside. Most Democrats are still angry and seething and this is why they hate George W. Bush or any conservative candidate for that matter. Sadly, during the few years that the Republicans held both the Senate and the House, as well as the White House, they, like their counterparts, got fat at the trough of government spending.

Newt Gingrich, (whom I met one time in New Hampshire,) began to clearly define the battle grounds of this culture war and for the first time the American people began to see that most Democrats are on the wrong side of just about every social issue in America. How can this be? What happened to the great society we were promised? The New Deal? Everything was supposed to be so good; I don't understand. We found out way too late that the FDR socialist approach of government handouts will not work; they never have and they never will. More government handouts and programs only mean more workers depending on the government for work who in turn create more government programs and that, my friends, becomes a bureaucratic nightmare leading to socialism. Open borders leads to more votes for Democrats which, (as we see) drives this country deeper and deeper into socialism.

I had a conversation with one of my favorite uncles; the now departed Frank Dagostino, not long before he passed. "Uncle Daggy", as we called him personified the American dream. The son of immigrants from Italy, Daggy worked his way up from nothing to become a successful vice president of Merrill Lynch and eventually passed on his business knowledge and hard work ethic to his son Joe and his grandsons Anthony, Frank, and Joe Jr. Not too long ago cousin "Frankie" collaborated with Donald Trump in a building property venture of some sort. Anyway, Uncle Daggy could not stress upon me enough that day how important it was for me to rely on my government Social Security. I could never figure that one out. In 2004 and 2005 President George W. Bush made overtures that our soon-to-be bankrupt Social Security system was in need of repair. You would have thought that President Bush had suggested the mandatory drowning of cute little kittens. The riot-like reaction to such a suggestion was completely disproportionate to reality. The truth is that our government has been spending the Social Security money in this elaborate Ponzi scheme for many years. There is no "lock-box;" there is no "security" in this social program. The strange part about the upheaval the President and others caused is that the ones who would NOT have been affected, were the ones who complained the loudest. Like my Uncle Daggy, older folks were foaming at the mouth just at the mention of some degree of privatization. As a side note, in my opinion, social security will only be "fixed" when a President of the United States (in the first year of his or her second term,) makes "fixing" Social Security, a national priority! Soon the 2006 elections came around and the idea was dropped like the political hot potato it was. I received similar reactions from people whenever I addressed this issue on my radio show – but why? I think I finally figured it out. Now I could be wrong, but to this day, I still believe average, older, citizens, cannot fathom that the United States of America could mislead them, plain and simple.

With the birth of the *nanny state* mentality via the "new deal", FDR told us Social Security was a good thing, and so many believed, it must be. It's known as the *normalcy bias*. I really think that those who do not hold a strong religious belief, but otherwise have a high level of patriotism, replace their "patriotism" as their religion of choice. This is exactly how Richard Nixon was run out of office, the idea that a PRESIDENT of the UNITED STATES could or would do something unethical or unlawful was unthinkable to so many. Skipping right along, my, how times changed from that mentality of thinking the government can do no wrong to Bill Clinton lying to us. The average older citizen, like my Uncle Daggy, just cannot wrap his mind around this, even as it happens right before our eyes. Of course, we are finding out now that many Presidents and Governments have lied to us over the years, thinking it was for "our own good." Don't be surprised if you find the next Democrat elected President using and abusing executive privileges in an attempt to keep this entire financial mass together. Doing an end run around Congress via Presidential executive privilege will be too much temptation to too much power.

I think we are just now starting to see the same effect on people who are coming to grips with the issue of illegal immigration. As plans are being made to incorporate Mexico, Canada, and the United States into one big North American continent, the average citizen cannot comprehend that a sinister plot (if you will) has been in the works for years. This is a plan to build super highways and erode our national identity and citizenship, as a way to stave off an incredible trade deficit and borrowing pattern from China. According to Professor Laurence Kotlikoff, a leading constituent of the US Federal Reserve, the United States is heading for bankruptcy. In his paper Kotlikoff states that a "ballooning budget deficit and pensions and welfare time bombs could send the economic superpower of the United States into insolvency." **Source: Telegraph.CO.UK**

This potential merger with Canada and Mexico may be the only "out" today's globalist politicians see for us in order to stop our potential economic collapse and ruin. Of late, "progressives" like Ted Kennedy, Hillary Clinton, and yes – even Republican members of the Council on Foreign Relations – have become more emboldened. Take, for instance, Teddy Kennedy. Much has been written about the "Kennedy curse," starting with Daddy Joe Kennedy all the way up to the most recent DUI of Congressman Pat Kennedy. I won't add to what has already been written except to say I probably agree with almost all that has been written and said. Joe Kennedy typifies what happens to man when he says he loves God and in real life does so much contrary to the Word of God and God's will. There is no doubt that, as a whole, the Kennedy family is very "religious," but where I come from, it's not what you say that makes you who you are, it's how you act and what you do The character of a man is what he does or does not do in SECRET!

The insatiable quest for power Democrats have, is nothing less than covert evil! In reality, there is not even an attempt by the Democrats anymore to hide their lusts for power. Senator Schumer's hearing that broached the subject of using abortion as a "litmus test" for selecting judges. Senator Jim Webb, (D-Va) threatening to 'slug' the President of the United States; for his stance on the Iraq war; Nancy Pelosi, childishly flexing her grand mom muscles after being elected Speaker of the House, and her ill-advised and "traitorous" visit to Syria in April 2007, are all classic examples of which I speak.. The culture war is here – not in the future – and its battles play out today!

The Bible is equally clear that Rodney King's rhetorical question "Can't we all get along?" is pie in the sky utopia. The answer is an unequivocal "NO" – we can't all get along. There are radical, Muslim extremists in the world today who at best want to rule the world under

Sheria law and at worst, desire to see you and all things American and Israeli, DEAD! Dee-Eee-Aai-Dee, dead. They want you dead; they want your grandchildren and your children dead. Nothing short of your spilled blood is their desire in life. So much so that many in the militant Muslim and Palestinian communities begin teaching children their brand of "religion" – to hate and kill Americans, Christians, and Jews. We have two choices with them: convert or be killed. How many more will have their heads chopped off before we wake up?

Why do they hate us?

Scholars can do a much better job of telling you about Ishmael and his half brother Isaac than me. Both were the sons of Abraham in the Bible. Isaac, born to Sarah, became a "father" to the nation of Israel, Ishmael born to Hagar, became a "father" to Islam. The Bible says that Ishmael: *Will be a wild man; his hand will be against every man, and every man's hand against him; and he shall dwell in the presence of all his brethren.* **Genesis 16:12** There are additional reasons that go beyond the blood lines for the hatred of the United States by Islamic fascists. They hate us because our Judaic-Christian concepts equate to freedoms they will never understand, much less be willing to grant, especially to women. Couple that Judaic-Christian concept with our support of the Nation of Israel and the second reason for their hatred becomes no more complicated than that.

They also hate us because, in contrast to their religious beliefs, our freedoms allow us to live in a culture of lustful images bombarded and saturated with "soft porn images." Without the ability to combat the spiritual side of lust and sin, the Islamic answer is to cover women from head to toe! This is the exact opposite of the Christian approach that says that only Jesus himself can change a blackened heart. They hate us because we offer freedom and liberty, given those "freedoms," most people choose the temporary, the sin, the lusts of life over the straight and narrow. In the mind of radical Muslims, "our way" simply does not work. And… they hate us because we are or were financially blessed in this country by God. Keep in mind; most of the ancestors of these radical Muslims were nothing more than goat and camel herders until our glut for oil made them billions and billions. I believe that hard financial times are getting ready to befall the United States it may bring this great experiment in freedom and liberty to a close. After that, just as we are seeing the radical homosexuals win at almost every level, soon the "progressives" – the Hillary Clintons, the Obama's, the Nancy Pelosi's, and the Charles Schumer's of this world – will eventually gain power again and believe me, when they do, with the help of the main stream media, they will NEVER give it up. They all use the *Saul Alinsky* playbook! Although Democrats like Pelosi, Schumer, Clinton and Obama are consummate "appeasers" when it comes to enemies of the United States. They have no problem fighting to maintain their own power or the use of military force globally when it suits their end game. Don't be surprised if you find a Liberal President one day, suggesting the use of military power to accomplish an end to a progressive means. Currently, they will do or say anything to occupy the White House again. In our short 231-year history, we have gone from allowing the SELFLESS to the SELFISH, run our country into the ground. Politicians with integrity are now the exception rather than the rule.

It never ceases to amaze me how soldiers in the Revolutionary War could just stand in a straight line all the while they were firing and being fired upon. If you have never seen the movie "The Patriot," starring Mel Gibson, you need to see it. I would like to see that movie made mandatory viewing in every high school in the country. It was their character, their sense of duty and honor; they were doing the right thing.

Now, what about you? You have a duty to go back to God! A former pastor friend of mine (Tim Smoyer) had a similar A.W.O.L. experience but, having reported for duty, not only was he punished but many looked at him as they do me – with a distrusting eye and always with a "traitor" mentality. Get used to it! Do your job for the Lord in spite of what they think. Those around you, those pastors you knew, you already know many are not your friends, but they are still your brothers in arms! If you're serious about getting back in the Army of God, accept the fact that many will never fully trust you again. This is still no excuse not to perform your duty as an officer in the Army of God. Like it or not when you raise your hand in the military and join, you are in! The moment you take that oath to "protect and defend the Constitution of the United States" you're in. In the case of military services you're only in for a period of years. When you asked Christ into your heart He took you seriously; how long have you been A.W.O.L.? What's that you say? You never prayed and asked Christ into your heart? What are you waiting for?

So when congregants or the media start questioning your sincerity, stand tall. Mean what you say and say what you mean. Brainwashed? Cult? NONSENSE!!! By becoming "CHRIST-LIKE" we get to share in the blessings of a king's office. Make no mistake about it, being next to our Commander in Chief Jesus Christ is better than being near any president, senator or movie star we could ever hope to meet – trust me, been there, done that! How many armies are there where privates and generals alike get to sit with the king?

If we are not governed by God, then we will be ruled by tyrants. William Penn

Obedience is Better than Sacrifice

The Bible says that obedience is better than sacrifice. As we enter the millennium, in light of 9-11 and perhaps on the brink of World War III, I believe any thinking person should take the time to reflect on his past. The past makes an excellent benchmark, a road map if you will, for life; none of us has an excuse to stay off course.

As I said earlier, people do not want to face the inevitable. I suppose I have seen enough death and dying in my life to fill several people's lives. I used to boast that as a volunteer rescue worker I saw more blood and death by age 17 than most people see in a lifetime. It's probably still true today. Having reached what I determined to be the half-way point of my life, I'm determined to make the second half of my life much better than the first.

So, after all these years, it has finally sunk in and I have realized and learned the importance of obedience and that it is in fact better than sacrifice. I think I fully understand now what Saint Paul meant when he talked about turning someone over to Satan so that his soul might be saved. One of two things will happen, either the person will come to her senses or (I believe) she can be lost forever. If a person is seeking the truth, sooner or later he finds his way out of the prison camp and starts his way home!

Did you ever see a war movie where, in one moment one soldier will be talking to another, and then in an instant a bomb lands and one of them is completely blown away, gone, missing? That's how I felt for a time – I was the guy who got blown up and the next thing I knew, I woke up here. What happened? How did I get here? Where are my friends? My "curse" was my "success." My "success" only served to make my "fall" even harder.

As I said, what amazed me was finding out the level at which government officials, including district attorneys, will go to eliminate or at least discredit "Christian programs" and ministries. I'm not just talking about Janet Reno and the federal government killing innocent children at Waco and Ruby Ridge. I sure don't compare the injustices I suffered to be on the same level as these extreme examples. But I do point this out as alarming in the wake of many civil liberties that are being taken away, using the war on terrorism as an excuse.

The case of Anne Sutton is so typical of the nonsense Deborah and I had to endure. Anne Sutton is the daughter of the late Rod Sterling, creator of the sci-fi show 'The Twilight Zone." Anne's husband Doug was falsely accused until a court-ordered psychiatric evaluation finally concluded the girl that made the false charges was suffering from a delusional disorder and her allegations "were patently false." *NY POST* 10/13/03

Chapter 9
IS SOCIETY PLAYING GOD?

As I said earlier, there are certainly more dramatic and heart-wrenching stories about 9-11 than those from my family and me, but these are the kinds of life-changing experiences more and more people are going to experience in the coming days. The churches are not ready for the influx of those who will be coming to them for help or guidance. We really have very little time in the great scheme of things. We cannot be responsible for whether the churches are ready or not. It is our job to be ready on an individual basis; trust me, God will take care of the rest.

This is not a how to "gain" Christian book. This is a hard look at how the Lord is always trying to improve the quality of our lives. Using my rollercoaster life as an example, I hope you begin to realize how God is always drawing us closer to Himself. If you believe in God, why is it so hard to believe that He intervenes in people's business today?

My Circle Theory

Actually, it's not my theory at all. I heard Dr. Charles Stanley explain it once and have heard others since then. I heard him explain that God has certain life steps laid out for our growth and development. The book of Romans bares this out, perhaps the subject my next book. These are steps that help us learn, grow and mature. Very often in Christian circles we will take a person who has lived a life wrecked with sin and with the most vile, destructive outrages. When this person comes to accept Christ publicly as his personal savior, many pastors will make the mistake of parading the born again person front and center – as living proof of the miracles of God. This is intended to change the hearts of men. It's especially true of Christian television and radio where young producers, hoping to impress their bosses, book these guests who, unknowingly, get great inner satisfaction from knowing they are loved and accepted. For sure, God does change the hearts of men and women and He is still doing it today. Too often we have seen these rock stars, athletes, abortion doctors, famous people who had been doing the "Devil's work" come to Christ and then be promoted among Christian circles. All too often, many of them disappear months or years later. Never fully being able to meet the standards we wrongfully set up for them and not knowing how to proceed, they go back to what they know best, a life of sin, never to be heard from again. This is why the Lord never requires we take on more than we can handle.

Baby steps are the order of the day from the Lord. The Bible talks about learning, "precept by precept," line by line, a little at a time, if you will. **Isaiah 28:10**. For the Christian these steps are permanent and irrevocable. As I said earlier in this book, I don't think the teaching steps of the Lord ever leave those of us who seek His will in our lives. These steps are designed for our growth, our well-being, our need to "be conformed to His image." I have often said and believe that the more we become Christ-like here on earth, the less change needs to take place when we get to heaven. It seems to me that when we do cross over to the other side, there is a purification process, a point where, prior to entering Heaven, all those ungodly habits and sins must be burned off – a final cleansing process if you will. If I'm right, then it stands to reason that the more we are "Christ-like" here on earth, the less spiritual change needs to be done as we enter through the pearly gates.

HOW?

How do I give up smoking? How do I give up viewing bad television or web sites? How do I give up that "thing," that sin that nags at my soul? I will say this from my own experience, four realities have helped me in my own struggles against my "sins of my flesh."

First, realize that you are not alone. We are all human and we are all susceptible to our sinful nature and the "sins of the flesh". Yes, when you were saved you became a "new creature" in Christ Jesus. You were unplugged from your sin nature, but it is the job of Satan and your own flesh, aslo the world in general, to reconnect you to those sins. Recognize your failure(s). *More on this to come...*

Secondly, (*and most importantly*), remember apart from the cross of Christ we our powerless to overcome our worldly desires and fleshly nature. I'm not talking about two beams of wood stuck together, or a trinket hanging from your rear-view mirror, or a tattoo on your back. When I say the "Cross of Christ", I am referring to the power that comes to a Believer through the death, burial, and resurrection of Jesus Christ.
For the law of the Spirit of life in Christ Jesus has made me free from the law of sin and death. **Romans 8:2**

Third, repentance is the key. The word "REPENT" actually means to turn away, <u>you must be willing</u> to turn away from this sin that plagues you, every day, every hour or every minute, remember, Jesus had to die for that sin, TURN AWAY! He is more than willing to help you turn away if you are willing to sincerely ask Him.

Finally, every time you slip (and you will,) ASK GOD FOR FORGIVENESS! Ask the Lord to take the desire for this "sin" from you, HE will. Ask Him to replace the things that are of YOU with HIM! I have found it useful to remind myself, that this sin (whatever it is) is NOT God's will for my life. God will honor your bended knee to Jesus in your desire to be obedient.

1. Focus: on Jesus John 14:6
2. Object of faith: The cross of Christ Romans 6:3-5
3. Power source: The Holy Spirit Romans 8:1,2&11
4. Results: Victory Romans 6:14 *Courtesy JSM.org

When I was a child, I spoke as a child, I understood as a child, I thought as a child: but when I became a man, I put away childish things. **1 Corinthians 13:11**

When I was a kid I played "Army" or "Cowboys and Indians", maybe you played "Barbies?" You don't play "Barbies" anymore, why? You simply outgrew it. The same will happen to you as a Christian. When you repent, ask for forgiveness and draw closer to God through Prayer, Bible study and church attendance, God WILL help you put away those childish sins that so beset you! What the Lord requires of us, He will provide FOR us! So yes, I believe the Lord sets up steps of growth for us. I believe that no two people's steps are identical in order of God's priorities. This really negates our ability to judge one another based on what WE believe someone else should be doing or not doing. As an example, you may have come to Christ and He may have instantly delivered you from cigarettes. Now you are on the Lord's step six or seven and come across a person who has been saved for many years yet you see her smoking a cigarette. You gasp in horror because this Christian should know better. In judging that person we make the most common mistake in all of Christianity. For you cigarettes may have been step number one or two but, for that person, the Lord may feel it's more important for her to stop lying or stealing or to stop cheating on her husband. Why do you think Jesus spent so much time teaching us not to judge one another?

God decrees the steps of growth in each individual, not people as a whole. I can think of no better example in the Bible of this than John chapter 21:21-22 when one disciple pointed out another disciple to Jesus and said "what shall this man do?" In other words, what about him? Jesus could not have been more plain in His answer when he basically said: you worry about you and let him worry about him. In other words, mind your own business, I'll take care of him. How many have been driven from churches because of people's need or desire to impose man-made standards on others? Yes – we all grow in the Lord at different rates through different experiences and this requires different steps for all of us. I honestly believe (for the Christian anyway) that God continues to bring us around in a circle to similar circumstances in life so that we may learn from our mistakes and progress. It's one of the reasons why we see people getting married three, four, sometimes five times. The Bible talks about people returning to their own sins as a dog returns to its own vomit. **Proverbs 26:11**

The faces may be different, the locations may differ, but many of us – if we take the time to observe – will realize that we seem to be creatures of habit going in a circle. I believe this is simply God's way of urging us to correct and improve our lives. Too often, we make the same mistakes with the same results. It's been said the definition of insanity is doing the same thing over and over again, expecting a different result. We progress by learning from our mistakes and moving on after correcting them. I can tell you (and you'll read how it happened again more recently) there have been several times in my life when I have lost almost everything – job, house, car, reputation, you name it. In 2004 we finally filed for bankruptcy. Each time I seem to be down, I end up with a common, (tent making) type job of some sort only to be elevated by God to a bigger or better position of help or ministry of some type later on. It seems God always puts me on the bench for awhile before He puts me back in the "big-game."

Nevertheless, that could just be me. I will tell you, regardless of your situation and the steps that God has laid out for our personal growth, to the Christian at least, this "circle theory" holds true. To a degree, we would all prefer to skip steps and get directly to the finish! If you are like me, you would love to skip over steps three and four and get right to step five. I used to believe that God would not allow us to skip those steps and get right to step five. But my experience has taught me a little differently. Surely the Lord will allow you (if you insist) to skip certain steps to your growth and development in HIM. But here's the downside. If you skip ANY steps, you do it by your own volition; you do it at your own risk!

Whatever it is in your life that makes up step number three or whatever step you may have skipped over, HE will bring you back to correctly take that step sooner or later, i.e. the circle theory. God may be dealing with you about anger issues, jealousy, a need to feel superior by putting others down around you – the list is literally endless. Your own motives and maneuvering may have led you to believe you overcame missing steps, but God was not fooled!

From a heart of love and compassion, the Lord brings us full circle in an attempt to have us complete the steps HE knows we need in order to fulfill our calling from on high. As I said earlier, the faces and places may change but the circumstances will be identical or at least so similar as to remind the thoughtful of God's gentle yet sovereign hand upon our lives even today. How many relationships have you had where you just kept falling for the wrong kind of person? How many of us repeat the same non-productive behavior year after year, over and over?

"I WILL BE LIKE THE MOST HIGH"

How art thou fallen from heaven, O Lucifer, son of the morning! How art thou cut down to the ground, which didst weaken the nations! For thou hast said in thine heart, I will ascend into heaven; I will exalt my throne above the stars of God; I will sit upon the mount of the congregation, in the sides of the north; I will ascend above the heights of the clouds; I will be like the most High. **Isaiah 14:12-14**

These verses, perhaps more so than any other, capture the crux of Christianity and its God-centered philosophy as opposed to our natural inclination for self-centeredness.

I saw a woman in Tucson, Arizona, wearing a black tee-shirt with bold white lettering that simply said; **IT'S ALL ABOUT ME**. Isn't that the sad truth in society today? When Lucifer decided he was going to assault God and make his kingdom like God's, he used an awful lot of 'Is.' "**I** will ascend into heaven, **I** will exalt my throne, **I** will sit upon the mount, **I** will ascend…**I** will be like the most high." In other words, I will be my own God. The Christian philosophy, however, requires a deliberate "death to self."

For those desiring to understand more about the Creator God, even our thought life becomes subject to God's standards. How many of us would like God to hard wire our brains so that every thought we think, ends up on a giant TV screen for the world to see? As you go through life it should not come as a surprise to find yourself in similar circumstances over and over again. You may not find yourself back at your own personal step three or four, or nine for that matter, as a result of anything you did or did not do. It may be that you find yourself here again because of your wrongful motives or thinking; every one of our situations is different, yet the Lord deals with each of us in much the same manner, He is no respecter of persons!.

WHEN YOU ARE READY TO SURRENDER, then you get promoted!

I hope most of you saw the movie "Saving Private Ryan." If you did not see it, you are missing a great one. It is said to be one of the most accurate movie portrayals of D-Day in WWII in all of movie history. I can only assume this is true, having heard many WWII veterans on TV who were actually there, saying that the movie is in fact accurate.

Please indulge me while I veer a bit off course and tell you a true thing that happened to me the first time I saw the movie. At the time I lived in a small rural town that had an old-fashioned movie theater, the kind I grew up with but is rarely seen these days with all the mega theaters showing 18 different movies at the same time. With the paint peeling off the walls and ceiling, the old style chandeliers were huge and probably had not worked for many years. If I had to guess I would say that this particular theater in Souderton, Pennsylvania, was probably built in the late 1920s or '30s. The first scene of the movie is enough to glue anyone to his seat; I don't think any scene in any movie has captivated me more. At the end of the movie, there is another scene that equals or surpasses the first. During that final battle scene I sat upright, glued to my seat, not able to take my eyes from the giant screen or even eat my popcorn. As I sat, eyes wide open, taking in every move intensely, something crawled up my arm. It may have been an ant, a spider? To this day, I still have no idea. I did not even pay attention to whatever it was that was crawling up my left arm. I simply remember grabbing it with my right hand, crumbling it a bit and throwing it down on the floor. It was not until the movie was over that I remembered doing this and, as I said, to this day I don't know what poor little creature gave up its life because I was too engulfed to pay attention. Now that's a movie! If you saw the film, you will recall that the first battle scene opens with soldiers in some type of platoon boats coming in off the sea ready to hit the beaches. The doors swing open to unload the soldiers in about 15 feet of water (remember they are carrying 80 lb. backpacks). Bullets start tearing into the platoon boats and men are being cut to shreds. Many start diving over the side of the boat and drown because of the weight of their backpacks. Some manage to get the packs off only to have a bullet rip through their body while they are still submerged. The countless bullets flying from the German machine gun nests protect the beach like a warm blanket of lead, piercing every inch at one time or another. There is no place to hide. Iron structures designed to stop American tanks from taking the beaches were strategically placed for maximum effect. These iron structures could barely give one soldier cover from the barrage of bullets. In the movie it appears anywhere from six to twelve soldiers try to hide behind these structures. Several times, you can see men taking other men's dead bodies and positioning them to afford just a bit of cover from the rain of bullets. At one point, the hero, played by Tom Hanks, gets behind one such structure while he and several other men are preparing to continue their assault. Tom Hanks plays the captain, yelling instructions for his sergeant (we will talk a little more about sergeants later). At another point a young private yells at the captain and basically says "you're crazy I'm not going anywhere." The Ping-PING sound of high-powered bullets can be heard ricocheting off the structure every few seconds. Now at this point the captain can only do a few things, one of which is to threaten the private with a court martial. Believe it or not, "desertion" in wartime is a capital offense. I doubt seriously that public schools even teach about Private Eddie Slovak anymore. On the other hand, he could have done what I would have done. Stuck a pistol in the soldier's face and tell him if he did not move up the beach I would shoot him myself! Surely, that would motivate even the hardest skeptic. But the captain played by Tom Hanks did neither of those. What he did do was calmly point out to the lad that *IF* he stayed there, he was surely going to die. By this point, the German machine guns were picking off GIs left and right. Think about it, stay here and surely die or at least have some control over your life and circumstances by taking a chance and moving forward.

  This whole scenario came to me one morning during those back-slidden years. I was considering telling someone I was prepared to surrender to my sin. to give up, to start living my life the way I wanted to and the hell with any consequences. To give myself over to sin and think that "surely God must have made me this way," I would have been believing a lie from the pit of hell! My sins may not be the same as yours. It doesn't matter what the specifics are. If you are in the enemy's camp like I was, you already know there is sin in your life. Too weak to give up the sin that beset me, I was ready to surrender and, to an extent, I did – until those immortal movie words played in my head – "If you stay here you'll die."

It's at this point that "good people" in the service of God move!

Literally in the movie and figuratively in life, the captain yells his orders to the sergeant, the sergeant verbally kicks his men in the butt, and they move to the crest where the beach meets the land. Unfortunately, the German machine guns are highly elevated on small cliffs that border the land and the beach. Our problems have not gone away.

Let me warn you, the minute you take a step of renewed faith towards the Lord, you risk being blown to pieces. You'll be the victim of spiritual gunfire, land mines, hand grenades, or any number of things will be thrown at you, <u>and that's just from the people that call themselves Christians!</u> The enemy is going to throw things at you as well. The only difference between being in God's army and any other field of battle is – we don't have to worry about actually being blown to smithereens! God does sustain us even when we walk through the valley of death. That's where you or somebody you know is right now: in the valley of the shadow of death! It looks like we can get killed. I've been there, alone and afraid, but you make your legs move even if you have to pick them up with your hand, one step at a time. If you think you are not ready now, you never will be ready. This is war, **MOVE UP THE BEACH!**

How did I get that weak? It started with the sin of pride.

My sin of pride got me arrested.

My sin of pride earned me the front page of every newspaper within 50 miles of my house, including the *Philadelphia Inquirer*.

My sin caused eggs to be thrown at my house and to have my kids tormented in the neighborhood.

My "miscalculation," as they call it in the Army, caused no fewer than four houses to go up for sale on my street. Several times we caught reporters snooping through our trash.

Ask my two youngest daughters how the Lord delivered their two best friends to that neighborhood during that time. Blessings for my children caught in the middle of the firestorm. To this day Sarah and Stephanie are still friends with Falyn and Caity. Two neighborhood girls who became best friends with our daughters – what a glorious answer to our prayers for the kids!

Yes, my surrender to the enemy when I caved in made me a deserter and caused me untold sorrow and poverty. In our neighborhood, our closest neighbors never really gave out interviews about us. Maybe they just did not want to get involved, or maybe they supported us – either way, Deborah and I were always very appreciative. We would often comment about how we got warmer receptions from people who did not claim to be "believers" than those who did.

This is one of the reasons that I played so much racquetball during that time – even going so far as winning a state "mixed doubles" championship in 1999 with my second partner, the affable Judy G. I found that "non-believers" in racquetball circuits accepted me for who I was and how I treated them, without concerning themselves with the validity of any charges against me. Heck, even two of my racquetball buddies, Steve and Marta Griffith, a married couple, came to visit me one time when I was in jail. That meant a lot to me; it was refreshing and healing to say the least. I thrived in this "non-judgmental" environment. If only we could transfer the same love and acceptance to our churches.

When I was in jail, I refused to allow my own children to come see me. Maybe that was a prideful thing too, but I did not want my beautiful and innocent children to ever have a mental picture of their father in jail. How many "Christian" friends came to visit me? ZERO! Two pastors from two different churches, Glenn Serino & John Battaglia, but no friends, none of the other pastors I worked with, only my wife Deborah. I'm leaving out the prank calls, the hate mail, the time my wife was snubbed at a Christian women's AGLOW meeting and numerous other indignities we suffered. To say the least, we were living a horrible nightmare. Nevertheless, as bad and as real as those things were, they are only a SHADOW of death. I'm still here and I still have the most wonderful family on the face of the earth. My absolute faith that God will preserve my family as long as I don't turn myself over to my sin (again) is what keeps me trying to work my way "UP THE BEACH." Don't stay where you are and die!!!!! Work your way up the beach soldier – get moving now!

Chapter 10
THE BREAKING PROCESS

Whoever falls on this stone, will be broken: but on whomever it shall fall, it will grind him to powder.
Matthew 21:44

Navy Seals have a slogan – "That which does not kill you, will make you stronger." Sometimes when we are going though the "breaking process," we want to look up at God and say "I'm feeling strong enough now Lord!" If you have ever experienced God's breaking process then you know it's true; 'that which does not kill you WILL make you stronger!'

Paul, from his prison cell, wrote,

Being confident of this very thing, that he who hath begun a good work in you will perform it until the day of Jesus Christ. **Philippians 1:6**

So, why is it that when Christian brothers or sisters like Deborah and I go through tough times, other "Christians" feel a need to bite or gnaw on us with their words? They are known as "JOBS (*pronounced=* ***JOBE'S)*** Comforters." Jobs Comforters are people who judge other people that are experiencing bad times. They reason among themselves that their MUST be some secret sin at play? Many in churches today are far too quick to scoff and scorn, instead of trying to see God at work – in spite of what they perceive to be another person's faults! Job experienced the full wrath of this doctrine; it's a fascinating read in the Old Testament. Having been guilty of this myself for so many years, I am amazed now that I never saw it in me.

People who have been kicked when they are down need encouragement not scorn. They need to hear that any day things are going to get better for them. ... ***the goodness of God leads (people) to repentance..***" Romans 2:4

That's not optimistic hype or unrealistic, hyper-faith double-speak. It's factual. It is NEVER God's desire that you walk through life bloodied or beaten spiritually. The good news is that once you have been through the process of breaking you will know the elation that comes when you and God finally have a breakthrough. You may not even feel those chains that wrap around you like a boa constrictor, but when you are loosened from those chains of bondage, you are free indeed! I cannot describe the exhilaration I have witnessed and felt myself.

While living in D.C. I also wore the hat of the Director of Communications for the Traditional Values Coalition. It turned out that behind the scenes, this "ministry" is as phony as a three dollar bill, more on that in a minute. It took me a long time to see that first-hand, however, and I did gain some tremendous experience while I was there. I read 18 or 20 newspapers a day, scanned untold Web news services, and watched different television news channels often simultaneously in order to keep up to the minute on current events. Although I did not know it at the time, this practice, to a degree, would eventually be the foundation of expertise I would need in broadcasting my radio show every week. By the time I got home in the evenings, there was not much time for recreational television. I spent as much time and energy with my family and their activities as I could. Never enough for Deborah, sometimes too much for the kids – what-are-ya-gonna-do?

One evening, Deborah and I were watching a television show that had two segments in it. These two points perfectly sum up what I am trying to say in regards to God's BREAKING PROCESS. The first segment of the program dealt with Jim Bakker, former head of PTL, and his son, Jamie Bakker. I have not read either one of their books but from what I saw on television, I realized that Jim, Jamie, and I have a lot in common. While I was riding high back in the late '80s and early '90s, Jim Bakker was having a nervous breakdown right there on television. People laughed at him in droves, and that was just the Christians! I remember writing him a letter at the time and in fact, he did write me back. A few years later, I was to find myself at the bottom of my valley. I probably would have had a nervous breakdown except I escaped inside a bottle. Thrown in jail for 74 days for a crime I didn't do. As I said, I didn't know then what I know now – it was for a reason. I was running from God and God will use many different means to get our attention if we don't learn the lessons we need to the first time around.

Jonah is the quintessential example of a man who didn't listen to God and got himself in over his head before he came to his senses. Listening to God (again) has given me blessings upon blessings. While watching that segment about Jim Bakker I saw that people, especially Christians, can be very unforgiving when our brothers and sisters get knocked down. I think a lot of the disdain people feel towards the "weak" comes from a fear that they may one day find themselves in similar bad situations. Hate what you see? – stay far away from it and "it" will never happen to you. A nice theory but hardly realistic. Everyone and anyone has an opinion of why things happen the way they do, but who are we to question when God 'disciplines' his children? We should look at it as Isaiah did –

Woe to him who quarrels with his Maker, to him who is but a potsherd among the potsherds on the ground.

Does the clay say to the potter, 'What are you making Does your work say, 'He has no hands'? **Isaiah 45:9**

It can feel so lonely when we are going through that dark process of being re-made. Many make the mistake of giving up, when often; the "promised land" is just over the crest of the hill. That brings me to the second segment of the show my wife and I watched on television program. That segment was about Russian Detachment Syndrome. For those of you who do not know what this is, I will try to explain. This "syndrome" originated in Russian orphanages where babies are sometimes raised from birth with very little or no human interaction or contact. They are just left in their cribs for days on end with little touching other than having a diaper changed or being fed. To some degree, these children spend the first four, five, even six years of their lives in isolation. They are oblivious to love, emotion, and feelings of any kind from humans other than themselves.

When the Russian Mafia saw the business opportunities that could be had from placing these children for adoption, the orphans began finding their way into the homes of American couples desperate for babies. But these children are far from what we would consider "normal." They have the potential of pure evil. They aren't necessarily evil to others; mostly they are destructive to themselves. They do "weird" things like throw themselves down staircases, bite, mutilate, burn themselves – anything just to feel something. This is a result of growing up with virtually no love, feelings, or emotions. When love is absent, evil takes its place. Until you've experienced total isolation, until you've been cut off by your own people, until you've had no contact with those in the church whom you thought cared about you, until you feel no one reaching out, no God, nothing – you cannot understand how dreadful it feels.

For Deborah or any woman, I think the "heart pain" someone goes through when they experience something like we did is probably tougher than most people care to admit. For me it was more of a fight against the bitterness and resentment that stirred within me. To this day, probably the hardest part of dealing with my ordeal is conversing with someone or working on a project of some kind and then having that person begin to avoid me, not return my calls, or in general, create distance between us. In my experience this has been a direct result of something that person heard or read that somehow made him suspicious of whether I was actually guilty – in effect, thinking I might be lying to him about my past. Or, the person just hears about the false charges against me for the first time and 99% of the time when that happens, the person – usually calling himself a Christian – never has the courage to ask me directly about what he read or heard. They simply choose the path of least resistance and stay away; it still frustrates me when it happens.

Your circumstances may not be specifically identical to mine, but the way people who are down get treated by others is typically very similar. Ask anyone who has lost a loved one and he will tell you that many people offer support in the beginning, but after some time passes, many times it seems as if those who were so supportive start to drift away. When you reach that point, however, you have two choices – become bitter or become better!

Jim Bakker had to learn this as did I. The isolation and rejection were some of the darkest days for my family and me. At times we swore God was nowhere to be found. But HE was there

If I make my bed in hell, Thou art with me **Psalm 139:8**

I just needed to get off my "high horse" and turn to face the music. God brings us through a breaking process in order to make us into the men and women He desires us to be so that he can use us for His Glory. How we react to HIS guidance determines how quickly we learn and how quickly HE turns things around for us. We are not always responsible for the things that happen to us, but we ARE responsible for how we react to those things!

We have a choice as to how far we are going to let Him go. We will have numerous breaking processes through our lives but it's up to us if those will be the same lessons we have to learn over or if God can move on to teaching us greater things about His identity. If you are going through a dark time right now, I hope and pray that something you are reading is moving you back. Moving you to escape the enemy's POW camp; moving you to use the God-given time you have left to store up your treasures in heaven where moth and rust cannot corrupt!

Playing God

The LORD said, 'Behold, the people is one, and they have all one language; and this they begin to do; and now nothing will be restrained from them, which they have imagined to do' **Genesis 11:6**

When God said this, He certainly did not mean it as a good thing – however, HE MEANT IT!

I taught a lesson years ago about that verse and have never heard a similar sermon from anyone else. It seems timely and ties together several points scattered throughout this book. The teaching was about the Tower of Babel, and said, there is something deep in the words of God – God never speaks just to be heard. EVERY WORD God utters in the Bible has deep meaning for He has a profound interest in our well-being. It amazes me how different Bible verses can contain different, deep meanings for different people, yet it's final interpretation and direction always remains constant. Being made in God's image is the ONLY reason why we are special. Many times we forget this and tend to think that our "special-ness" is based on how many achievements we have or don't have.

Yes, the Lord expands your coast when you ask Him to. An excellent example of this is found in a very unremarkable place in scripture. Right in the middle of a listing of the sons of Judah are three verses that give your eyes and mind a rest from reading all those hard to pronounce names. The verses speak of a man named Jabez and a brief but powerful prayer he prayed that God used to bless him in a tremendous way.

And Jabez was more honorable than his brothers, and his mother named him Jabez saying, "Because I bore him with pain." Now Jabez called on the God of Israel, saying, "Oh that You would bless me indeed and enlarge my border, and that Your hand might be with me, and that You would keep me from harm that it may not pain me!" And God granted him what he requested.
Chronicles 4:9-11

(There's an excellent book out that goes into detail about this prayer, *The Prayer of Jabez: Breaking Through to the Blessed Life* by Bruce Wilkinson. Don't make the mistake as some have of making this prayer an incantation. But if you haven't read it, you should. Back to the Tower of Babel – as wrong as the men building the tower were, they were not necessarily "evil." They probably thought they were doing "society" a favor. They could have started out their project with the very best of intentions – no one knows for sure – but there must have been something wrong because God chose to take action against the building. He must have had a good reason – God never does things just for His own entertainment – unlike what those who are bitter with God believe. He does things for our own good. He "confounded their language," stopped them cold – why? Surely that tower was nowhere near as tall as the Empire State Building, was it? I have no idea, however I do know this – God said: " …**and now nothing will be restrained from them."** Think about that. God is saying if these guys get to finish this project of theirs, "nothing" will be held back from them? That's heavy considering this took place a couple of thousand years ago! Whatever man has been trying to do in that regard, since the fall, he has, if only unknowingly, tried to be like God. Why do you think the Lord had to place an armed guard at the tree of life? He did not do it because it looks cool; there was something to it! Why did God stop the building at the Tower of Babel? Here's my theory – As men built the Tower of Babel, a historic building designed to reach the heavens, there must have been some "power" or "access" they were getting close to. Why else would God find it necessary to look down and stop them? I think we were, and perhaps are again, on the verge of reaching into that access or "power." Mortal man is not yet a spirit body. It takes a "spirit man" to deal with infinity, as it exists in outer space. What makes our reach into infinity any different today? I am not talking about reaching up to the heavens via the Tower of Babel or trying to colonize the moon or mars. I'm talking about "inner space." Reaching further and further into smaller and smaller particles, we are unknowingly "playing God." Has there ever been a time in your life when you have attempted to "play God" in a certain situation? Thinking you had everything under control; you had all the answers to the everyday problems you face only to have it all come crashing down around you? That is exactly what the people that built the Tower of Babel ended up doing before they even realized it.

I don't blame them anymore than I blame Adam and Eve. Are we so foolish as to think that "if Adam and Eve had just not sinned" you and I would not be going through the horrible times we sometimes go through? Nonsense! Adam walked with God, talked with God, and he still sinned against God. Do you think you are any better than him? You are fooling yourself if you think you are.

Romans 5:14 If you are like me, many times I was totally out of God's will, and yet was extremely successful! Success is no more a barometer of a person's "spirituality" than failure. People can get blinded by their own success. That was me! Moving in the "name" of the Lord, but not doing what the Lord actually wanted of me. Now on a broader scale, we can see nations rising up and "playing God" just as the builders of Babel attempted to do thousands of years ago. Can we think that God will not bring judgment on us just as He did on those people?

What do you mean "inner space", you may be asking yourself? Science is taking us into realms that we would have never thought possible ten or twenty years ago. Medicine is spiraling to new heights. Doctors have found ways to perform robotic heart surgery without opening the entire chest; we can clone animals and soon humans and human body parts. We split atoms almost without giving it a second thought. Soon scientists will discover the dark matter that holds the universe together. This why preliminarily they have called this dark matter; "the God particle". However, as I write this, man is getting ready to split more than atoms. Currently steps are being taken to create "Frankenstein Foods," the first mingling of human-origin genes and those from plants. They say these foods can be used to treat children with diarrhoea, a major killer in the Third World. Think about it, human genes in the food we eat! I'm thinking it is not such a good idea. Do you remember how much "POWER" the human race gained when it reached into infinity and split the atom? I fear the human race is on the brink of a similar release of power from stem cell research, genetic modifications, and cloning, but it is not a good thing.

As of this writing, to my knowledge, nothing good has come from **embryonic** stem cell research. This research involves an embryo, a "potential" life, ended in order to properly harvest the much-needed stem cells. Rather – and I admit limited knowledge here – all of the medical benefits that have come from stem cell research have been of the "donor" or "adult" variety. The stems cells that have shown the most promise to date have come from a variety of methods, including harvesting from umbilical cords and blood plasma. Actor after actor, however, has taken his cue from the late Christopher Reeve and would have you believe that somehow George W. Bush and the United States government is holding back the cure that may have helped Mr. Reeve walk again, nonsense! The poor guy probably got taken for what money he had remaining, and with his and his wife's premature deaths, their children were probably left with relatively nothing to speak of.

Scientists have already claimed to be able to clone human beings. In 2004 Panos Zavos, a reproductive scientist, announced in London that he was the first to clone a human and his paper was published in July of 2006. "Dolly," the first cloned sheep, was number 277 in the experiment because the previous cloned animals had a tremendous amount of defects. Genetically modified animals and vegetables are now becoming common-place.

How many babies are going to die deformed before they get human cloning right? These "cloned" babies will not be from fertilized eggs. Scientists now claim they can fertilize eggs without a sperm donor. Actually, they will be the result of genetic engineering from extracting DNA and implanting it into a cell, then charging it with electricity to make it divide and grow. Now they are talking about embryo farms – conceptual baby farms harvested for the "betterment of mankind." I don't think so. What makes any of us think we can play God? Do you think these cloned babies will have souls? I guess we'll know in the not too distant future.

I don't bring up the Tower of Babel as an individual matter suggesting great study. You can study it for yourself if you choose, of course, but I bring it up to show that we as "the church" need to get the message out. The further we get from God, the worse things are going to get in this country and in the world. Spiritually speaking, that is a small measure of how I feel the world is in relationship to a massive take over of "evil" that is going to happen soon! They are already talking about a National I.D. card or a chip placed inside our hands. Dare we not believe the Bible when this finally happens here? If my observations are correct, this "evil" is approaching the earth and is expeditiously speeding up the end time in Bible prophecies that we have all heard about. I of all people am in no way qualified to offer a theological, Biblical explanation for this massive wave of evil about to hit us, but I only challenge Christians everywhere to examine the signs in light of their own understanding of Bible prophecies. Do your homework, or ask your pastor, but whatever you do, don't just ignore things!

I DIDN'T REALIZE UNTIL I MOVED TO WASHINGTON HOW BAD THINGS ARE GETTING.

There is no time to talk about it anymore. The time to act is now and many Christians are just not equipped or confident as to what they should do. That's why I was so blessed by my radio show – I was actually able to help people again, a VERY good feeling! There's a book out called *See You at the Top* – not the top of the Tower of Babel, the "top" of life or so the author reports. I don't agree with Zig Ziegler on a lot of things but Zig does have a unique way of saying things. In this book, Mr. Ziegler talked about how to cook a bullfrog, stating that if you throw a big old bullfrog in boiling water, he's strong enough to jump out, a little worse for the wear. However, if you put a bullfrog in soothing water you can gradually get him so tired he will fall asleep and cook to death. Like the bullfrog, patriotic Americans and the church today are falling asleep in this country. We are so busy doing our own thing; we cannot be as powerful as God intended us to be. When I lived in Souderton, Pennsylvania, I finally attended two different church services after several years of not attending church anywhere. The two pastors were told, 'If Steve Aiken is going to go to this church, we are leaving.' One pastor stood up for us, the other pastor, well, not so much.

One of the main reason I started this book was to tell the church it does not know how to help wounded soldiers. Most churches failed us miserably in that department. They were either unable or unwilling to be a part of our healing process. Don't get me wrong, there were some pastors who tried to take an active role – some, but not many and not enough.

As mankind rushes head-first into a global economy and a global one-world government, without knowing it or saying so, mankind is rushing headlong into deeper rebellion against God. I repeat: **don't just sit there, get involved!** Don't be afraid. Help a political campaign, paint your church, join the rotary club, help a little old lady put her trash out every week, something, anything, just get involved. As Christians we are an army to be reckoned with! That fact alone causes me to jump to my feet and get back to "fighting the good fight." How many years should you wait? How many years have you been waiting? The Bible says: *...now is the accepted time; behold, now is the day of salvation.* **II Corinthians 6:2**

What are you waiting for? An invitation? A rescue party? It's not coming, each of us must take the initiative on our own to do what is right.

Society today still tries to set up barriers or hurdles for those who have fallen, dangling forgiveness and RESTORATION like a carrot on a stick in front of them, or making their "support" conditional. Nonsense!

The proof of whether a fallen, bruised, or hurt individual can or should get back in the game is directly proportional to his or her relationship with God. In other words, it's none of our business. That does not mean someone who is successful is necessarily blessed. Being successful sometimes, means just that, you're successful. Being blessed of the Lord allows your light to shine! Personally, if I have not learned my lessons, dare I go back in the good fight? God forbid! However, if on the other hand, you feel called, would it not be a sin for you to stay? This is all I'm saying! When you reach a point where you are willing to be held accountable, when you no longer carry around offenses against anyone, when you don't get upset if you don't get your way……….THEN you are ready!

Chapter 11
MY RADIO SHOW

Living in Tucson, Arizona, since December of 2001, I had a radio show called "Straight from the Hip" which was one of the highest rated, if not THE most listened to, talk shows in southern Arizona on the weekends. It was an uneven blend of religion and politics that struck cords at all levels. I attacked issues like "gay-rights," out-of-control government bureaucracy, gun control, abortion, and, of course, illegal immigration.

Me, live on the air

On the issue of out-of-control government, I would expound on cases like Wally Klump, arrested and jailed for many months for having his own cattle graze on his own land. He was jailed by the Bureau of Land Management and held in contempt. On a national level, Bob Schindler told my listening audience that I was the very first talk show host in the country to interview him. This was long before the story of his daughter, Terri Schiavo, made national news when the state of Florida allowed her to starve to death at her ex-husband's wish. I have been told by airline pilots that I was "an integral part in getting the pilots armed" (after 9-11). Yes, for a dinky little radio show in southern Arizona we had a lot of "firsts." On air, I would often talk about cases like the Sherburne family. A sad demonstration of how far out of line our own government – supposedly a government "of the people" – can go.

*Like millions of other Americans, the Sherburne family of Hesperia, California, owned a family business, selling clothing, survival foods, and military souvenirs at gun shows and swap meets. A Christian family, the Sherburnes had their faith in Christ put to a test starting on Good Friday, April 10, 1998.

April 10, 1998: The San Bernardino County Sheriff's Department – led by Detective Harry Hatch and Deputy John Lawrence – conducted a raid on the Sherburne home in Hesperia, California. Trudy Sherburne and three of her six children returned home one Friday evening to find law enforcement officials milling in and about the house and grounds – along with a newspaper reporter and representatives of the fire department, code enforcement, and the bomb squad. Soon thereafter, the police used their own explosives to destroy, with great fanfare, an undeclared quantity of what may have been the Sherburnes' merchandise in the backyard. (No one outside of law enforcement knows what was destroyed since the Sherburnes were not allowed to observe the proceedings.)

Trudy was arrested on charges of possessing a destructive device, deadly weapon, and child endangerment. Her three boys were taken by Child Protective Services (CPS) and turned over to their pastor's custody, over CPS objections. Trudy spent Easter weekend at the Victorville Jail. Her home and property were left open and unattended. A warrant was made out for her husband Chris's arrest, who was working in Florida with Trudy's three other children. (They were restoring a boat with an eye toward helping in the Sudanese Christian relief effort.) The *Daily Press*, a local paper, published a picture of a great explosion along with stories of the Sherburnes' "hoarding" and "stockpiling" a "cache of military explosives" and possessing warheads, missiles, and rockets. The assistant D.A. was quoted as saying "he believed the couple was using the property... as a storage facility for a militia organization." (Later in the investigation, FBI Agent Dan Bodoney was quoted as saying "...that there is no "hard evidence" to tie the Sherburnes to any illegal militia activities," and the *Daily Press* admitted no rockets or missiles were found.) Trudy was taken to the West Valley Detention Center in Rancho Cucamonga. At her arraignment, she was charged with six counts of "recklessly and maliciously possessing a destructive device." Bail was set at $1 million. Trudy, with no criminal record of any sort, didn't even know what the term "bail" meant.

     1. "NO CONTACT with any activist group or radical group or right wing group" – (Like the Boy Scouts or the Baptist Church?)

     2. Not to possess any activist, radical group or any right wing group magazines, which sell or depict the making or procurement of weapons..." – (Like *Field and Stream*, the *L.A. Times* or the Bible...?)

     3. You will NOT reside with or contact your co-defendant, Trudy Sherburne, while she is employed or involved in the business, sales, procurement, storage or trade of military supplies or surplus." ("NO CONTACT" means exactly that: "in any manner direct or indirect, personally, by telephone, letter, or through another person"-- which would probably include Chris and Trudy's children!)

4. "Not to participate in the sales of or act as a middle man for the transaction or sales of military supplies (surplus) of any type." The Sherburne family never received one food stamp or welfare check while pursuing their family business, in an industry that legitimately employs hundreds of thousands of families just like theirs.

The Sherburnes have been involved in a totally legal family business for years – the selling of military surplus and survival foods. In order for Chris to be released from prison, the rest of his family must forfeit their living in order to have any contact with him. Under this high level of control, any police officer, in good or bad faith, might arrest Chris and the violation could roll over onto Trudy, leaving their children without both parents again. Chris did not sign and thus did not legally bind himself to these parole conditions. His family, to protect themselves from over-zealous parole officers, would need to keep their own father far away from them. Any (perceived) violation of these incredible conditions would be monitored in what has been called "the highest level of parole supervision." December 1 Parole release date. Chris is not released for refusing to sign amended conditions. Chris, in pro per, filed a Writ of Habeas Corpus with the Superior Court in Blythe. Such writs require the "jailer" to prove the prisoner is lawfully detained. February 2000 Chris refused to sign the new conditions unless the "high control" status, potentially endangering his family, is removed. April 23, 2000 Board of Prison Terms Revocation Hearing. Parole revoked. June 11-12 Trudy is finally allowed to visit her husband. June 14, 2000 Chris is ordered to report again to A-yard Headquarters and is issued his fifth "Serious Rules Violation" for exercising his statutory right to appeal his parole conditions. For not signing his papers:

1. He remained incarcerated 15 months beyond his court sentence, with no credit being given to his discharge date. 2) He was sent to a "Level three" violent offender yard (with a 24 hour a day, seven days a week gunner).

3) Besides the approximate thirty hours per week of no pay labor he does for the Prison, he has also been ordered to do almost 100 hours "Extra Duty."

September 27 Court grants Trudy's petition for early termination of probation. Her felony is reduced to misdemeanor; her guilty plea was reversed. February 14, 2001 Board of Prison Terms revokes Chris's parole again (for the 7th time) and ordered a psychiatric exam. March 14, 2001 Chris files a Writ of Habeas Corpus with the Blythe Superior Court in pro per. It is denied without "opinion" in response to almost 100 pages of alleged & documented "grounds for relief," as was his appeal to the Fourth Appellate District, Division Two. The Supreme Court of California refused to hear his Petition for Review on October 25, 2000. By March of 2001, Chris has been held in Chuckawalla Valley State Prison in Blythe, California, for 23 months beyond his parole release date. He is considered a parole violator and duly punished as such by parole revocation, extra duty assigned, time added. He exhausts administrative remedies in seeking to appeal parole conditions. *end

I have no idea where this horrible miscarriage of justice stands today. Waco, Ruby Ridge, Project Megiddo, the Sherburnes… if you don't think these types of travesties are happening with more frequency in this Country, you are sadly mistaken. Since 2001 I have not spoken to anyone related to the Sherburne case, but I can assure you one of two things have happened since. Either they have disregarded their faith and are (perhaps bitterly) continuing to try and piece their lives together, or they would stand up and tell you that as bad as the things they went through were, God did bring good about from their most horrible experience. My guess is they are standing strong!

When the Nazis came for the Communists,
I remained silent;
I was not a Communist.
When they locked up the Social Democrats,
I remained silent;
I was not a Social Democrat.
When they came for the trade unionists,
I did not speak out;
I was not a trade unionist.
When they came for the Jews,
I did not speak out;
I was not a Jew.
When they came for me,
there was no one left to speak out.
        Pastor Martin Niemöller (1892-1984)

    The Sherburne case, Wally Klump, U.S. Marines chained up like their terrorist counterparts at Guantanamo Bay were exactly the kind of 'talk' the ministry side of my radio show was designed to expose.

    On the issue of illegal immigration, I really need to thank my listeners and especially my former friend Russ Dove for bringing me up to speed on the issue itself. Maybe it was just the timing but I would often comment on the air how those of us who grew up in the East did not consider illegal immigration to be any sort of a problem in the United States. It was not until I started to live through the devastating effects that I began to realize how those who support "open borders" are truly an enemy of the United States, hell-bent on destroying our sovereignty and making null and void all those who went before us, sacrificing their lives so that we can remain free.

Chapter 12
LEGALLY WHACKED!

Those of you who know anything about the Mafia, or have ever watched "The Godfather" or "The Sopranos" know the term 'whacked' means to be assassinated. Figuratively speaking, that happened to me on Friday, June 16, 2006 – the day I was legally whacked for my work in politics.
 Going back to 2001 for just a moment, a former friend of mine, Phil Sheldon, oldest son of the Rev. Lou Sheldon of the Traditional Values Coalition (TVC), arranged for me to move to Washington, D.C., and go to work at the Traditional Values headquarters. I honestly believe Phil was sincerely motivated to help me get out of Pennsylvania as I was still having a hard time finding decent work after my conviction. Phil's wife Betty (not her real name) had actually spent time with Harriet one of the girls who falsely accused me and she was convinced my so-called "affair" with this young lady was a complete fabrication. She surmised that this girl had a transference of some type, equating how "nice" I treated her with a strong desire to have a "nice" relationship with a man. Betty did have a conversation with one of my attorneys, as did Phil, and both were willing to testify on my behalf at my trial. Why my "hot shot," know it all, Philadelphia attorney never called them is beyond me.

 Anyway, on at least one occasion, I slept over at Phil and Betty's house as Phil gave me odd jobs around his house to help me pay my bills. Not long after that, one of their two sons – severely handicapped – passed away, and through lengthy conversations with Phil, I did my best to bring comfort to both him and his wife. It was not long after that Phil approached me about going to work for his father, Lou Sheldon, in Washington, D.C.I knew "Rev. Lou" in passing from when I was in charge of security or body-guarding Beverly LaHaye at various Christian functions around the country. Actually, this seemed like it was going to be my dream job as my official title was Director of Communications for the organization. That same year I registered as a lobbyist because I attended many meetings with members of Congress, mainly to work on President George W. Bush's first piece of legislation, the Faith-Based Initiative known in the House as HR 7.

HR 7 essentially declared that non-profit organizations which do good work – such as drug and alcohol rehabs, homeless shelters, and soup kitchens should not be denied access to federal funding simply because these organizations had a religious foundation. Through this legislation, organizations like the Salvation Army and Teen Challenge would be placed on an even plain with their secular counterparts. I spent a great deal of time at Congressman J.C. Watts's and Tom Delay's offices, and in meetings with low-level White House staffers – all in an effort to see HR 7 get passed.

Former Speaker of the House Bob Livingston

The big day arrived and we were told to expect a vote around 10:30 that morning. By three that afternoon, with no vote in sight, we finally got word that there was a major hold-up. I was told that Congressman Jim Kolbe (R-AZ 8) and several other representatives were willing to hand their own president a major embarrassment. By denying President Bush his first piece of legislation, legislation he had campaigned on and had promised conservatives nationwide, Kolbe and his cronies knew they could position themselves in a power play to get concessions for other matters of higher concern to them.

"Jim Kolbe, who's Jim Kolbe?" was my only response upon learning of the log-jam. Dozens of us hit the hallowed halls of Congress, the underground railway, congressional offices, stopping congressmen on the street just to get them to consider a "yes-vote" on HR 7. Twice I collared my own congressman, Joe Hoeffel (D-PA 13), and tried in vain to get him to vote yes. After all these months of hard work and endless hours of meetings, at about 11:30 that night we were told that the speaker of the House Dennis Hastert had struck a deal with Jim Kolbe and portions of HR 7 would finally be passed. It was late, we were all very tired, and I remember just whispering a prayer – "Lord, I don't know who this Jim Kolbe is, but if I can ever be allowed to pay him back for this hassle, I'd sure like to." Be careful what you pray for!

Traditional Values Coalition…*doing the "work of the Lord" on the outside, greedier than greed on the inside.*

I worked for the Traditional Values Coalition for much of 2001. I actually lived on the third floor of the headquarters on C St., 932 feet from the lawn of our nation's capitol. The deal was that I would work for almost no money. In return, I would receive housing and the ability to stay and work in Washington, D.C. Deborah and I decided to take the offer as we considered ourselves "Christian missionaries." The move motivated me to continue my sobriety and to try and patch up our marriage, a marriage that I had managed to almost totally destroy.

After a few weeks of living in D.C. and commuting back to Pennsylvania on the weekends, we took the plunge and moved our two children, Sarah and Stephanie, to Washington while our oldest daughter Mindy continued to attend Bible College in upstate Pennsylvania. Sarah and Stephanie shared a bedroom on the third floor of the main house in D.C. while Deborah and I moved in to a very small cottage at the back of the property. The deal was simple really, Sarah would attend a private Christian school with Andrea Sheldon's stepdaughter and her tuition would be included as part of our "salary." Stephanie, our youngest, would continue to be home-schooled, and all of us would work in the office at various times and capacities, being paid only food-money as we really did consider ourselves Christian missionaries, working for a Christian organization.

The more I became familiar with the organization, the more I began to realize that in my opinion, the organization primarily serves to line the pockets of Rev. Lou Sheldon and his daughter Andrea Sheldon Lafferty. I began to see first-hand how they would attach themselves to various conservative causes, surely those who make donations to theses various "causes" would be shocked to know just how little of their hard earned donations actually help the "crisis" of the month at TVC. I'm talking less than pennies on the dollar, hundreds of thousands of dollars, maybe millions.

For me it started with the myth that the Traditional Values Coalition "represents" over 43,000 churches. If that were true, it would make them more than the paper tiger organization that they are. I would be willing to bet that TVC could not come up with a list of these mystery 43,000 churches if it tried. If it ever could actually list 43,000 churches, I'd also be willing to bet that most if not all of those churches would be surprised they are listed as having ANYTHING to do with Rev. Lou or Andrea Sheldon. I never personally witnessed anyone at TVC commit a criminal offense however, what they do, and what they did to my family and me in the end, should definitely be considered "criminal." Aside from the 43,000 church myth, I witnessed them solicit donations for various accoutrements. If you gave so much money they would do this or that for you, of course I never saw any follow through. TVC received hundreds of thousands (perhaps millions) of dollars in the name of the Boy Scouts of America – money I am certain never reached the hands of the trustworthy, loyal, helpful, friendly, courteous, kind, obedient, cheerful, thrifty, brave, clean, or reverent. The Traditional Values Coalition took in hundreds of thousands of dollars (again, perhaps millions) in its crusade against NAMBLA, the 'North American Man Boy Love

Association.' Although I was completely unaware of it, TVC was raking in big bucks in the name of a young ten year old boy in Boston named Jeffrey Curley. Jeffrey was killed in 1997 by two perverts who took a page right out of the NAMBLA playbook to lure Jeffrey to his sadistic, untimely death. One of the perpetrators admitted performing necrophilia on the boy.

As part of my duties at the TVC, I met in Boston with Jeffrey's father, Robert Curley, then a Boston city fire Captain. The lunch Mr. Curley and I shared and the story he told shook me to my core. I returned to Washington, D.C., and began putting together newsletters and press releases that only continued to line the pockets of Andrea and Rev. Lou Sheldon. I seriously doubt that even ten percent of the money TVC took in, ever reached the Curley family at all.

As I became more and more suspicious of the actions of Andrea Sheldon Lafferty, I had several phone conversations with Martha Brant of *Newsweek magazine* and met her once in her D.C. office. At that time, TVC was using a mock-up of a *Newsweek* cover in order to raise funds for its "Boy Scout Crusade" to allegedly HELP THE BOY SCOUTS fight against the attacks by radical homosexual organizations.

Andrea began sifting through all of my notes, my computer, and anything else she could find at TVC headquarters. At Christmas time 2001, I was summarily fired from the TVC. That created a PR problem for Rev. Lou as we had no money and we were living on his "ministry compound." Rev. Lou did not want the bad publicity that would inevitably come by throwing us (literally) out on the street. However, that was just not acceptable to Andrea who had her lawyers draw up papers against me. She not only falsely accused me of stealing various items, but she also tried to get a restraining order that would have kept me off the property and away from my wife and children. Thank God, the judge in that case, realized that Andrea was overreacting, so he gave us about 30 days to vacate the premises. We literally had absolutely no money and no place to go.

Not surprisingly, Andrea broke her word to pay for our daughter Sarah's Christian high school and did her level best to hurt and harm us in every way. She even had the phone in our cottage disconnected, which made it impossible to arrange to get out and away from her. Since my children were allowed to stay (by court order) in the main house, we ended up running a 200 foot phone cord from the main house back to our cottage. Plugging the cord in every night when Andrea left the offices and taking it out in the mornings before she arrived. I'm told that Andrea later either filed theft charges against me for stealing a computer disk (a total fabrication) or somehow got a judge to find me in contempt. I was never served with these charges nor am I certain of their validity. I can assure you, the Sheldons paid more money to their lawyers trying to discredit and ruin me than they paid my entire family and me the whole year that we worked and lived at their headquarters! Somehow word of the atrocious way this "Christian ministry" was treating my family and me made it to the Bill O'Reilly television show. I received a call from one of O'Reilly's producers and was asked if I wanted to come on and expose this debacle. A debacle created by Andrea Sheldon, with no legitimate reason other than a paranoid fear that her brother Phil was using me to get a foot-hold into the organization. Initially I agreed to go on the O'Reilly factor, until I spoke to Dr. Tim LaHaye. Dr. LaHaye asked me not to go on the show and of course, I acquiesced.

If the Sheldon's actually did file some type of charges against me, to this day I have no knowledge of it. I do know that in September of 2004, (three years later) I attended a briefing inside the White House, passing the security background check and entering the White House without difficulty. I also know that someone in "authority" needs to follow the money trail at TVC and ask some tough questions: Can you provide a list of the alleged 43,000 churches you claim to represent? Do these churches even know you consider them a part of your organization? How much money did you raise in the name of Jeffrey Curley? Where did that money go? How much did you raise to help the Boy Scouts of America? Who ended up with that money? Who is on your Board of Directors? How much say do they have in the daily operation of TVC? The list goes on and on. Unlike other Christian organizations I have either worked for or volunteered for, in my opinion, the Traditional Values Coalition is a sham.

That Christmas four great friends came to rescue our family: Penny Nance, former board member of Concerned Women for America and now working as a special advisor in the Federal Communications Commission Office of Strategic Planning and Policy Analysis; Pattye Meagher, former Communications Director to Congressman Walter Jones; and Tim and Beverly LaHaye. It was Dr. and Mrs. LaHaye who actually paid for us to move to Tucson where we had an apartment and a job waiting if I could just get out there! So we packed up our two teenage daughters, two parakeets, a cat and bunny into a U-Haul truck and drove almost 3000 miles to Tucson, Arizona. God knew what He was doing, but we sure didn't.

Tucson, Arizona
In January of 2002, I met Tucson Pastor Jim Hoogenboom. Pastor Hoogenboom is a great preacher who also should write a book of his own someday! To my knowledge "Pastor Jim" was the last US citizen to twice meet face to face with Yasser Arafat before his death in November 2004. Reverend Hoogenboom literally gave me thirty minutes of his radio time on a local radio station. This pre-recorded half hour of religion and politics did so well that the station owner eventually ended up giving me three hours every Saturday, telling a colleague that my show put his station on the map on the weekends. With help from Larry Osment Jr. the show quickly gained popularity and became the talk of the town in conservative circles. I was always very open and honest about my previous false convictions and never attempted to hide the fact, knowing that I was in the middle of writing this book and would talk openly about it for the rest of my life.

In 2002 I had a chance to interview Retired Colonel James Behnke. Colonel Behnke is a seven time Bronze Star recipient and was running for Congress in Arizona's eight Congressional district against – you guessed it – Jim Kolbe! The main issue for Candidate Behnke was illegal immigration. By then the adverse effects of illegal immigration in southern Arizona had shut down two trauma centers, was a direct cause of skyrocketing crime and increased pollution through trash and debris, and was taking its toll on an already over-taxed electorate that has to educate thousands of children who are in this country illegally. Mr. Behnke took an amazing 14,000 votes from Kolbe in that year's Republican primary.

Then Came Randy Graf
In 2004, former Majority Whip in the Arizona State Legislature Randy Graf gave up an opportunity to run for a

third state term so that he could run in the Republican primary against Jim Kolbe – a third term that even the liberal press conceded Graf would have won easily. By then Kolbe was lying through his teeth to his constituents, saying that "border security was his highest priority." Maybe he wasn't lying, maybe he just wasn't telling us that the "border security" he was referring to was Mexico's southern border with Guatemala?

It was for that 2004 Republican primary that I volunteered as Randy Graf's Communications Director. With no money to speak of and really just a good old-fashioned grassroots campaign headed up by Jim and Jenny Coniglio, I honestly believe we were on our way to unseating a ten-term incumbent congressman, known as the "Cardinal" for his seniority. Kolbe ended up spending over a quarter of million dollars in the last 30 days of the campaign, spreading nothing but lies about Randy Graf and scaring people into thinking Randy was determined to take away their Medicare and fire all teachers and police officers. Kolbe's campaign kept up the lies about Randy and with George W. Bush running for his second term, many voters took a "don't rock the boat approach to the election. All in all, Kolbe spent almost a million dollars hanging on to his seat. Graf spent just under 100 thousand dollars. That's right – the ten term incumbent had to outspend Graf 10:1 just to hang onto his seat! Not long after that Randy approached me and asked me to be his new campaign manager for the 2006 Republican primary. I knew Kolbe's votes and his sinister ways of campaigning like the back of my hand; I also knew it would be my greatest honor to God and my Country to see Kolbe removed from office and to help Randy Graf get elected. Although it meant about a $1,200 a month cut in pay, and losing my health insurance, I said YES!

I never had any doubt that Kolbe would use my past in some way to try to hurt Randy's chances for election. Although Randy and I never got into specific details about the false charges against me, we always knew we would probably have to deal with it at some point during the campaign. In April of 2005 Randy made the announcement that he was going to run again against Kolbe and I immediately sprang into action. I began by raising nearly $93,000 from donors who had given to the last campaign. With the help of Jake Barr of I-Rapture.com (a Web provider), and Todd Evans, a computer genius, we set up a special Web site, outlining many of Congressman Jim Kolbe's outrageous votes that showed him as the *forked tongue* politician he had become. For instance, people were amazed and angered to find out that Kolbe was the only Republican to vote against the ban on partial birth abortions! They were angered that he had written special language into appropriation laws making the Tucson Sector of the Border Patrol the ONLY sector in the nation not permitted to establish permanent checkpoints. (The Government Accountability Office later did a study stating that Kolbe's policies in Tucson made the Border Patrol 77% **less effective**.) Not long after Graf announced his intention to run against Kolbe, the 11 term Congressman put out several fundraising e-mails, stating:

As you may have heard, Randy Graf announced today that he is running against me in the 2006 Republican Primary. It is unfortunate for the Republican Party and the people of southeastern Arizona that, just a few months after the divisive political campaign of 2004, they are already being subjected to a campaign for an election that is almost a year and a half away. This announcement, at this time, shows a complete disregard for the people of southeastern Arizona and the Republican Party.

Nevertheless, we have beaten him before, and we will beat him again. And, ***I commit to you that I will again***

196

fight back with everything we have and more. We will win by much more because last year the people of southeastern Arizona saw the real Mr. Graf; his extreme views and his inexperience make him a bad fit for southeastern Arizona, unelectable, an individual who would be thoroughly ineffective in the US Congress...

Kolbe also immediately brought Speaker of the House Dennis Hastert to town for a fundraiser. Meanwhile, e-mails at Graf headquarters swelled into the thousands just in Arizona's Eighth District alone. A year away from the primary election we already had unstoppable, grassroots momentum. We, (Randy, Jade Stokes, Kathryn Harvey, Iris Lynch, Liudyte Baker, Dean Miller, and a handful of others) began to prepare folks for the onslaught of deception just in case Kolbe tried that route again. Our battle plan against Kolbe was simple: we would have him suffer *the death of a thousand cuts* as we continued to bring to light his own atrocious voting record.

We were also getting ready to advertise Jim Kolbe's membership in the **Council on Foreign Relations** (the CFR) – which had just put out a press release calling for no more borders between Mexico, the United States, and Canada by the year 2010. I suspect Kolbe ran a poll at that time but I cannot substantiate that. Kolbe knew he was not going to beat Randy Graf again, so he suddenly announced he would not be seeking another term and threw in the towel! My legs were shaking when I called Randy with the news: Kolbe was going to retire and not run again!

ANYBODY BUT GRAF!

As speculation swirled in the media about who would run for this now open seat – to our surprise – nobody stepped up to the plate to run against the "front-runner,"

Randy Graf. Kolbe did television, radio, and news interviews to try to do as much damage as possible and harm Randy's chances for election. The strategy began to backfire as Kolbe just did not know when to stop. The local media started picking up on the fact that Kolbe simply had a personal vendetta against Randy Graf. It's rumored that Kolbe joined forces with the White House to convince then Surgeon General and Arizona native Dr. Richard Carmona to run for his vacated seat. When the speculation about whether Carmona would run became rampant, none of the people mentioned by the media, county officials, former GOP bigwigs, state senators – I mean NOBODY! – had the courage to step up and declare he or she would run. It wasn't until Jim Kolbe announced on a local radio show that Carmona was not running did all of the "Johnny-come-lately's" start pouring into the race; now that's real courage and leadership for ya! *Cough-cough.*

Kolbe continued to besmirch Randy Graf, trying to convince anyone who would listen that Randy Graf was simply "too conservative to win the general election against the Democrats."

Jim Kolbe continued his scorched earth policy against Randy until one day he stepped over the line and declared that *the one person who could not win the general election was Randy Graf.* He went on to say that he had **seen all of the polling data,** *and that he [Randy] simply cannot win the general election.*

I HAD HIM!

I finally caught Kolbe in a lie and I could prove it. As Randy Graf's campaign manager, I set out to find reporters who would listen and challenged them to have Kolbe produce this mystery **polling data**. I knew it was a lie and that no such data existed but getting the local press to pay attention was another matter. I finally settled on sending out almost 10,000 e-mails locally, offering dinner for two to anyone who could show me the data. I did not receive a single taker and Kolbe never mentioned it again locally.

That brings us up to June 10, 2006. After working for Randy full time-plus for over a year, I finally decided it was time to take all three hours of my radio show and promote Randy Graf broadcasting live from his headquarters. Needless to say, the show was a huge success. At one point there was standing room only in Graf HQ and we were finally able to give Randy the time he needed to discuss the issues. He talked not only about illegal immigration but about all of the other issues that are important in a congressional race such as this: lower taxes, less government, helping veterans. Like Jim Kolbe, Randy's Republican opponents tried to convince the voters that they too were tough on illegal immigration. But not one of them was on the record as supporting Proposition 200 in Arizona which placed into law the requirement to prove citizenship to vote or receive social and welfare benefits. Randy Graf was one of the only elected officials in Southern Arizona to support the measure. One of Randy's Republican opponents, Steve Huffman, actually fought against the proposition. In spite of the millions of dollars that were spent trying to defeat the measure, it passed easily, carrying 57% of the electorate and over 47% of the Latino vote.

Congressman Kolbe's unquenchable thirst for power had him stab his old friend Mike Hellon, one of the other Republican candidates, in the back by endorsing Huffman instead. Hellon's ex-wife Toni Hellon was, at one time, Kolbe's campaign manager. Kolbe did everything in his power to appoint his own successor, Steve Huffman. Huffman had one of, if not THE, worst attendance records in the State House, missing 47% of the votes. Huffman, like Kolbe, was known for his dirty campaigning and just as I predicted months earlier, decided that he was going to make **me** the story in this election. Like Kolbe, Huffman spent hundreds of thousands of dollars replicating Kolbe's lies about Randy Graf but this time it did not work. In the end it was Jim Kolbe's **endorsement** of Huffman that was the "bacio della morte," Italian for "kiss of death," for Mr. Huffman.

June 16, 2006 – I received "the call" from Brian Ross, of ABC News. Mr. Ross is noted for his attacks on conservatives and is currently in litigation with Speaker of the House Dennis Hastert for inaccurate reporting.

I posted the following on my Web site:

Just as I Predicted
By Steve Aiken
June 17, 2006
*It's apparent that political operatives have used my past (of almost twelve years ago) to try to hurt Randy Graf's chances for election. On **March 25th, 2006**, I predicted on my radio show, ALMOST to the letter, that this was going to happen!*
Here are the facts:
I've spoken openly on my show about my past. The story about the arrest was first released on ABC. I asked several reporters who interviewed me if they could themselves pick up the phone and have ABC jump on a story as was done in my case. They all answered in the negative.
In theory – and this could just be me – a 22-year powerful Congressman who just happens to be supporting one of Randy Graf's opponents could most certainly make that kind of phone call.
Keep in mind, we had received inside information that Huffman was going to use my past to try to ruin Randy's run against him.

Huffman did the exact same thing to another radio talk show host in Tucson, John C. Scott. In that case, just prior to the election, he reached down into the gutter and (again) dug out the fact that when Scott was very young, he too had a conviction for a relatively minor offense. Huffman barely won that race. Do you see a pattern emerging here?
Now back to the broo-ha-ha surrounding me.
Within minutes of the ABC story coming out about me, Huffman put out a press release copying the story with mug shot and all. Heck, he wasn't even smart enough to wait until my body was cold. However, if the Left or even those of my own Republican Party think that this is somehow going to make me go away, they do not know me very well. I will not stop promoting Christian and conservative candidates and causes. I'm sure not going to curl up in a ball and go away just because I was falsely convicted almost twelve years ago. That is exactly what the Left and enemies of this great Country would like, and exactly why I will not cave in.

I must have done fifteen or twenty interviews that day. I was on my cell phone so much that the battery went dead. I think I surprised the media by answering their questions forthrightly and was not afraid to take the subject of my past on with them. I had spoken openly on my show about the false charges against me, and I had no problem talking about them in this venue. I did receive a call from one of the producers of the Alan Colmes (of Hannity & Colmes fame) radio show, but that was one interview I was not about to agree to do. .

Knowing Kolbe or Huffman were going to make me the story at some point, it had been my plan all along to take a lesser role in the campaign or leave Graf altogether. On many occasions, I reminded Randy that he "could always fire me." I did not anticipate having to leave until about 30 or 45 days before the primary. This is when I figured they would launch the attack on Randy using me as the ammunition (at least that is when it would have done the most damage). Regardless, I never planned on running Randy's campaign for the general election, but I was hoping to stay by his side in some capacity. I always knew it might be in Randy's best interest to let me go so that my past would not become a distraction to his campaign, and I was prepared. In the end, it was in Randy's best interest to "fire" me and I was more than willing to fall on my "sword" for the greater good.

What I was not prepared for was having the radio station owner cancel my radio show over this. Of course, the man is a Christian, and as I said, it's not strangers who can hurt you the most, it's often your own "brothers and sisters." I viewed the cancelling of my show as the most cowardly thing I had ever seen this man do. It took me a very long time to forgive him. However, I often said that it wasn't my show: it belonged to God, I hold no hard feelings. I was now faced with having to walk the walk and not just talking the talk. It hurt a lot, but I got over it

So, I was legally "whacked." They beat me but they could not beat God and they sure did not beat Randy Graf in the Republican primary! In spite of the lies Huffman's campaign spread about Randy, he beat Huffman by more than 6 percentage points! It really was my greatest honor and duty to my country to help rid the country of a deceptive politician like Jim Kolbe and to jump on a political hand grenade for a man like Randy Graf. *BOOM* goes the grenade and I have lost everything, AGAIN. No job, no radio show, and no prospects. As Star Jones said on "Larry King Live" after being fired from "The View, *I don't know what the future holds but I know who holds the future!*

In the latter part of 2006, rumors started to swell around Jim Kolbe and his own problems involving Congressional Pages. Just like Barry whom I wrote about earlier, it seems that people who go out of their way to hurt other people usually get their own just rewards sooner or later, some call it Karma, I call it poetic justice. For the rest of my life, I will cherish one of my highest honors, and that is that I helped a real "man of the people" like Randy Graf. In the end, the battle by "Republican elite's" to sabotage one of their own, (Randy Graf) and the mood of the country against President Bush and all things "Republican", became a losing proposition for Randy in the general election, he lost to the Democrat candidate.

Ridding the Country of "Disease"

Many accuse me of being vehemently opposed to the likes of Congressman Jim Kolbe simply because he is a homosexual. Perhaps this stems from the fact that I own the nation's first and only children's story book designed to **PREVENT** homosexuality, *Mommy, why are they holding hands?* ISBN 0-9663380-0-6 ©1996

I came up with the idea and received a lot of help from Carla Tuhacek, but the book was mainly written by Deborah Prihoda in Texas. Both Mrs. Prihoda and I have been labeled as "haters of gays" but nothing could be further from the truth. Actually, my first known encounter with a homosexual was a woman named Althea Fitzgerald. As a police officer, Althea was the first murder victim I encountered. She was killed by a jealous lesbian lover who paid a mentally retarded man to do the deed in return for sex.

When I arrived on the scene, I found Althea grasping for breath and clutching her chest that had received three stab wounds to the heart. As a small part of the homicide investigation, I witnessed first-hand a bizarre sex world that I previously knew NOTHING about. Years later, I would receive a college equivalent education from my good friend and brother in the Lord, Jim Johnson. Jim was cited in *People* magazine as being the first Christian to open hospice houses for dying GRID patients. Back then it was known as **G.R.I.D**. (Gay Related Immune Deficiency). Of course the politically correct left quickly had that name changed to AIDS. Much of the Christian Community owes Jim a debt of gratitude for his contributions in arming the "right" for debate. To this day, I have several friends who are practicing homosexuals. I do not believe that "gays" are born "gay" but rather I firmly believe homosexual behavior is learned behavior – learned by a failure to bond with the same sex parent and/or early childhood sexual abuse.

Exceptions to this belief are what I term "lesbians of convenience" – typically white females between the ages of 28 and 45 with 1.2 children, the LOCs hate men, having been left behind by one or more. They "hook-up" with another lesbian simply because their sexual needs are being unmet. There are also those sometimes known as LUGs: "Lesbians Until Graduation." Once again, they are typically white and experiment with homosexuality at college because it is the "in" thing to do.

In a broader sense this is why as a Christian Conservative, I feel obligated to try to expose the "madness" that is the radical homosexual community and its "disease-like" spread across our country. If homosexual behavior is not "learned behavior," why is the radical left trying so hard to indoctrinate our children into accepting their odd, sexual behavior? Let me state for the record, like most Americans, I have no problem with what consenting adults do in the privacy of their bedrooms. However, as I stated on my radio show numerous times, I draw a line in the sand when they continue to indoctrinate our children – using our tax dollars – in our public schools! We have reached a point in this country now where the battle to eliminate any sexual orientation or definition of the sexes is being won by the left. Here is an example as reported in World Net Daily:

Homosexual-activist cop threatens Christians

Officer orders pro-marriage petitions removed from Promise Keepers event A homosexual-activist police officer assigned to security at a Promise Keepers men's conference in Florida is being investigated for threatening members of a Christian organization petitioning for a state constitutional marriage amendment.
"I have never in my life seen such unprofessional and bizarre behavior from a law enforcement officer," said John Stemberger, the president and general counsel of the Florida Family Policy Council. "This kind of ridiculous harassment and intimidation was meant to thwart the effort to protect marriage in Florida. It should remind all of us that we are engaged in a culture war. …"
© 2006 WorldNetDaily.com *Used by permission*

© 2006 WorldNetDaily.com *Used by permission*

Sgt. Stephen Allen, right, kisses another officer to mock Christians (Florida Family Policy Council)

Or take the case of Nicholas Anderson in Broward County, Florida, as first reported in the *Broward-Palm Beach Times*. Nicholas is a five year old boy whose parents are forcing to live as a girl! In fact, the Andersons now call their son Nicole, dressing him up in female attire and insisting that the public school treat Nicholas as a girl using the girls' restroom and all. To the "progressive left" this is real societal progress and a real breakthrough for transgender children! In reality it is nothing short of lunacy in the extreme, perpetrated by "no-good-do good-ers" like the Andersons who take great pride in their "advanced thinking" and "child rearing." Legal child abuse by any other name is still wrong!

Woe to them that call evil good and good evil...
Isaiah 5:20

The idea that any five year old would choose on his or her own to be a member of the opposite sex is just ridiculous. Yes, the emperor really does not have any clothes on. However, there are scores of so-called therapists and experts who will gladly go on radio and television to try and convince society that this is all perfectly normal and that the Emperor looks really good!

What the National Education Association, the radical homosexual groups, and "progressives" like the Andersons are taking advantage of is a time in children's lives when the last thing they should be concerned about is ANYTHING sexual. Certainly there is a time in most young boys and girls lives when they will (and should) look up to same sex role models. For a young five year old girl to look up to her mommy who bakes in the kitchen or a young boy to look up to his dad who fixes the family car are in no way shape or form what makes that child a homosexual! Yet that is exactly the times in a child's life that radical homosexual groups, with the help of the National Education Association, try and do. They take youngsters as young as kindergarten and try and convince little boys who look up to football players or male role models that this in fact means they are gay! These are lies from the pit of hell and yet the far left fringe is becoming more and more "mainstream" as people like you and I do nothing to stop this madness!

The Catholics used to have a saying that went something like this: Give us a child until they are in 7th or 8th grade and they will be a Catholic for life. Author Leoluca Orlando from Sicily has written extensively about the Mafia in Italy. Some of my relatives told me that my grandfather (whom I have never met) was killed by the Mafia in a fireworks factory. Other relatives adamantly deny this; I have no way of knowing the truth. Anyway, Mr. Orlando said the total and complete annihilation of the Mafia is "close at hand" in Sicily. This is significant in world affairs only as it relates to the eradication of terrorism, however there is a role reversal study here as well relating to the radical homosexual movement in the world.

The eradication of the Mafia offers us a micro-insight into the desire to remove Christianity and Christians from the arena of ideas. Things like homosexual marriage are a benchmark in U.S. history that will expedite the rise of evil power in the world seeking to silence and ultimately eradicate Christianity from the world. It will NEVER happen, but a lot of "Christians" are going to be taken prisoner soon in this country. I don't mean in a physical sense necessarily, but I see more and more attempts to create legislation that erodes our right to free speech by way of "hate crime' legislation. I suppose the first prominent example of this in the U.S. is the 2004 arrest of the "Philadelphia 5." A group of Christians attended a "gay pride" event in center city Philadelphia, only to be arrested for holding up signs, praying, and singing songs on the sidewalk. Meanwhile the "pink angles" held pink Styrofoam placards in the Christians' faces and blew whistles in their ears. I personally have had fake blood spattered on me, condoms thrown at me, whistles blown in my ear, and been spat upon and attacked by radical gay activists. The arrest of the Philadelphia 5 in 2004 is the height of hypocrisy and the beginning of tyranny against Christians, conservatives, and anyone else who dares disagree with them.

I fear our Constitutional rights will continue to be watered down, just as the Mafia was eliminated at the local and national level (in Sicily). I believe when there is no longer a common enemy, the world will look around for one. My guess is that it isn't going to be homosexuals or Muslims. Trying to silence Christians and Jews has been the goal of the enemy since the dawning of time. We are already seeing it in Canada and European countries.

How did they nearly rid Sicily of the Mafia? They did it by "CIVIC EDUCATION!" In Sicily the children are taught Noi Simmo Uniti – We are united. United against what? The Mafia! School books in Sicily are filled with pictures of car bombs, twisted metal, wreckage, scary stuff. Hello? Is any of this sounding familiar? The school books also have pictures of very young little girls and boys with paintings and posters that say Noi Simmo Uniti and often the child will be pictured writing the name of a Mafia "Don" in his or her own handwriting. This campaign has been going on for years. Mr. Orlando is correct in his correlation of "Civic Education" to shaping societal opinions. For years, people like me have been telling anyone who will listen about the evils of "public education." These "evils" have been supported in part by a government that has helped foster an anti-Christian bias. We are very near a point in time where the victory by anti-Christian forces will be complete! Homosexual activists have been winning battle after battle for years. Radical homosexual think tanks have plotted out their strategy very well. The key to their ultimate victory will be in direct proportion to their ability to reach our children in public schools. With catch phrases like "there is no room for hate", "tolerance" radical homosexuals have stolen the language of the arguments and have wrestled the debate into the "civil rights "arena by implying that" gay rights, and "civil rights" are one in the same. As they continue to convince more and more teachers to teach their brand of tolerance, society becomes more and more intolerant of those who disagree with them, specifically Christians. How or why the black community allowed homosexuals to hijack the civil rights movement is beyond me, but hijack it they did. One only has to look at a recent decision in a Massachusetts federal court. In February of 2007 U.S. District Judge Mark L. Wolf dismissed a civil rights lawsuit brought by David Parker, ordering that there is an **obligation for public schools to teach young children to accept and endorse homosexuality**. What radical homosexuals have not been able to do through the ballot box or public appeal, they have been able to do through judicial fiat.

As I said earlier, other examples of this "Civic Education" for evil can be found in radical Islam where worldwide children are being taught Jihad, to hate Jews, non-believers, and Christians. It is the same long-term strategy being used by the National Education Association to indoctrinate children towards socialist political viewpoints, and it is working.

Chapter 13
FINDING YOUR WAY OUT

Training and Exercise.

Having had a good bit of police training, and a fair amount of martial arts training, as well as a plethora of bodyguard training, I would like to share with you the secret to training for anything.

I wish I could take credit for this golden nugget of truth but I can't. It was taught to me at the police academy by the finest professor I ever had: former FBI Agent Sam Bass, now deceased. Sam was a huge man – at least 6'4" and weighing close to 300 lbs. He taught us moves and maneuvers with only one designed purpose, staying alive in a crisis! I'll never forget that first day when Agent Bass, with his deep octave voice that was overlain with a heavy southern drawl, said, "It's a proven fact, in a crisis you will react the way you train."

If you train to fight, you'll fight. If you train to run, you'll run. If you don't train, you won't react or you'll freeze in a crisis. He went on to say that one split second of delay "COULD COST YOU YOUR LIFE!"

I was thinking about those poor GIs in WW II pinned down at the base of the cliffs – still being picked off but not nearly as badly had they chosen not to move. I once heard James Robison say, "In the Old Testament, the only thing necessary for the children of God to be in Sin was for them to not move when the pillar of God moved." **Exodus 13:21**

James Robison

Let me get back to the movie "Saving Private Ryan" for a moment. As I watched the scene, I was telling you about – the scene where the men are trying to make it up the beach – I remember my first thought was that; ***nobody could train for this!*** Yet our fictitious captain, as in real life, used his resources, in one case a "sticky bomb" he learned in the Army field manual.

When we are in danger, we tend to cling to the person with the most experience. In war, it is usually the sergeant and his experience. In danger, you cling to the person who has been there! If you are in spiritual trouble today, it will help to find yourself a "sergeant." Don't make the mistake of thinking this person – this "sergeant" or any person – is going to have the magic answer to your problems. He or she probably will not. However, find someone with some life experience who can support you. He or she is NOT the answer to your problem(s). If you become too attached to any one person who has been helpful to you, it is likely that sooner or later that person will let you down and whether that "let-down" is real or perceived, you'll find yourself back where you started. As I said earlier, no "human effort," no "will-power," by you or anyone else can take the place of the sacrifice and risen power of Jesus Christ at the cross. However, learning from others who have been where you are, is often times helpful and comforting.

The Apostle Paul said it so perfectly; ...*when I am weak, then am I strong*... kneeling at the foot of Jesus at the cross and receiving His grace is the only hope of mankind. My "sergeants" were Mike Jensen then Tim Smoyer – which led me to David Damiani – which led me back to my oldest and closest friend, Bill VanArtsdalen, then back to Matt Schiedel (after his release from prison). Remember we talked about point men? These guys ran point for me without even knowing it. Each in his own way had been burned by his own people, "Christians," and each made his own way back.

In the United States Marine Corps there is an elite outfit known as the 'snipers.' The snipers go through as rigorous a training routine as any other specialty units in the military. These highly trained, highly motivated, dedicated professionals do more than sit in high places and shoot bad guys from long distances. These Marine Corps snipers are often set deep within enemy territories because of their ability to hide and cover under all sorts of difficult circumstances and different types of terrains. They become the "point-men" for platoons and very often, they are sent on one or two men excursions to take out or neutralize various military targets of the enemy.

Picture if you will a dense jungle. You and I are on a two-person excursion. We are deep within the enemy's territory. In the past you and I have been very effective, we are successful, we are highly decorated Marine Corps snipers! However, as we go on more and more missions, you find me taking more and more risks. Because I am as good as I am, I don't listen to sound advice from elders in my field, not even you. In Christianity, the Bible calls this type of sin pride. In the military, the men who throw caution to the wind are sometimes very successful, and other times, like me, they trip, fall, and find themselves in an enemy prisoner of war camp.

As I said before, I mean no disrespect to anyone who literally risked his life in the service of our country. Undeniably the "Army of God" as a concept has been around for thousands of years. I merely tell my story in such terms to offer the easiest understanding and explanation.

Finding Your Way Out

Jesus wasn't kidding when He said, *In this world you will have tribulation.* Then He went on to say, *But be of good cheer; He has overcome the world"* **John 16:33** Once you accept the fact that **THERE WILL BE NO RESCUE**, by your "friends", your family not even your Pastor or church. You will begin to find your way out by realizing only God can save you! Here is the "secret" to finding your way out, realize that getting out is only going to happen when you surrender all to Christ! Only God can save you.

Beating that sin "thing"

As I travel and speak at various churches and men's groups, inevitably, either in person, or during the Q&A. Someone will tell me something like this: I'm a Christian, I know the scriptures about being a new creation in Christ, I know about old things passing away and all things becoming new! I know I have been Born-again, but why, why do I still struggle with this "thing" or that "thing?"

Let me begin by saying a resounding YES, if you have accepted Jesus Christ as your personal Saviour, by faith, you are a Christian! At times, you may feel like a hypocrite, but your "feelings" are of no consequence to this biblical fact! We are saved by Grace, not by "feelings" or "good works." You cannot give away enough money, you cannot help enough little old ladies across the street, you cannot read your bible enough, pray enough, there is nothing you can do to earn your salvation. It is God's grace that saves us, His finished work of Christ on the cross, a free gift, there is nothing we mere humans can do to earn it.

As I said earlier, you are not alone. ST. Paul the great Apostle who wrote three quarters of the New Testament said; *I do not understand what I do. For what I want to do, I do not do, but what I hate, I do* **Romans 7:15** He wrote this <u>AFTER</u> he became a Christian! He is describing, and goes on to describe, our "sinful nature" and it's constant desire to raise it's ugly head in our lives CONTINUALLY! Nowhere in the Bible are we ever absolved of our responsibility for our own sin. However, the fact remains, until you die and go to heaven, you are always going to be drawn to sin. Recognize that we all carry this "sinful nature," a preponderance and a predisposition toward sin! Like a flower drawn towards sunlight, like two magnets that attract one another, we are consistently being drawn towards sin. Some refer to it as the "dominion of sin" I prefer the term; "sinful nature". This is the concept you must understand before you can avail yourself of the "cure" which is only found in the Cross of Christ.

Every one of us has this "sinful nature" of which I speak. To the unbeliever it is the norm. To the Christian, this "sinful nature" causes great conflict and accusations of hypocrisy. Fear no person's condemnation(s), only you have to answer to God for you. The solution to the "sin nature" is found only in the Cross of Jesus Christ. When Jesus said:

"... *If any man will come after me, let him deny himself, and take up his cross daily, and follow me.* Luke 9:23

Jesus was not referring to asceticism, (the idea that one can attain a high spiritual and moral state by practicing self-denial, self-mortification.) He was talking about placing your faith in His Cross, only in the cross, and doing that on a <u>daily basis</u>!

This is nothing new, Paul wrote about the cross in one form or another almost exclusively. The entire Old Testament, almost exclusively, pointed people to the Cross! Yes, the Cross of Christ is what "saves" us, but its miracle working power is not limited to salvation alone. The Holy Spirit works exclusively in the life of a Christian by and through the Cross of Christ! It's called the "law of the Spirit of life", or the "law of the Spirit of life in Christ Jesus." It is the only "law" that CAN free you. The "law" of Moses cannot free you, "laws" or "programs" that you make up, or that were made up for you, cannot free you.

because through Christ Jesus the law of the Spirit of life set me free from the law of sin and death Romans 8:2

Your answer will only be found in making the Cross of Christ the object of your faith! Many Pastors today fail to recognize and teach that the Cross of Christ is most applicable to our sanctification, and not limited to our justification!

It also helps to come to grips with the fact that what you have been through, or what you are going through, is called **LIFE**. We have no control over the "cards" we are dealt. The Bible says that God rains on the just and the unjust. Matthew 5:45 We are also not responsible for what happens to us or how others act towards us, <u>we are only responsible for how we react</u> to them! Keep in mind that Jesus also said – not a sparrow falls to the ground that God does not know about. He is the God of the living and He cares about you as an individual.

Some will reach such a low point in their lives that they will sincerely say, "I wish I were dead" or "I want to die.'" I have dealt with dozens of suicidal people, (my mother-in-law committed suicide) – most of them really don't want to die, they simply want the pain to go away. Please don't think I am addressing this to someone who is bedridden and terminal either, I'm not. I'm talking to those of us that are still vertical! Move up the beach soldier, if you don't, you will surely die! This is where God comes in. As surely as you are reading this book, HE does care about you but HE cannot show you this when you are so wrapped up in yourself that you have become the center of your own universe. In this way (without realizing it,) you have made yourself your own god, a very bad idea.

The God of the Bible is very real. God cares so much for you that HE GAVE His only son. Ask me to jump in front of a train to save one of my children or grandchildren, and I would not hesitate for a second. But don't ask me to throw one of my children in front of that train, that I will not do, yet it is exactly what God did with Jesus on the cross – the ultimate sacrifice so that not only would you have blessings down here, but an eternity in

Heaven as well. Jesus said: *I go to prepare a place for YOU, if it were not so, I would have told you.* **John 14:2**

The evidence of your "cure" will come from changing your world from one that revolves around you, to one that revolves around the cross of Jesus Christ, as you minister to others even when they appear ungrateful. Believe it or not, it is then that you will find your way out. For me, just when I thought I was through with my own personal "breaking process" I learned quickly, well let's just say – *not so much!* THERE IS ALWAYS MORE TO LEARN!

And at the end of the days I Nebuchadnezzar lifted up mine eyes unto heaven, and mine understanding returned unto me, and I blessed the most High, and I praised and honoured him that liveth for ever, whose dominion is an everlasting dominion, and his kingdom is from generation to generation. **Daniel 4:34**

One Sunday morning in 1999, I awoke, feeling the best I have felt in many years (about six, I would guess). Arrested in 1995 and front-page news every turn I took combined with the gossip of the Christian community where Deborah and I had been forced to live wounded us so much more than I would allow myself to realize. There's an old counseling slogan that says, "Denial is not just a river in Egypt" and man I was swimming in it!

When you refuse to face your own sinful nature, your own shortcomings to any degree, much less the tons and tons I was carrying around, you are not going to want to see just how dirty you are! I guarantee you, my friend, when you see how dirty your own sins are, you never look at another person's tiniest faults, less you be reminded of your own big ones! **Luke 6:41**

I finally began cautiously lift my head up. Not so high that it's going to get blown off again, just high enough to realize I have been sitting on the bench too long. I felt like the guy sitting in dugout while his buddies played for the Championship. One of the things I learned while a spiritual POW was that some of my "buddies" were no buddies at all.

One day I did peek my head up just a tiny bit – after years of sitting on the bench. Did you ever sit on the bench in sports when other players you felt were not as good as you got to play more than you did? It's a terrible feeling, but in my case, it was nothing but foolish pride!

No wonder the Lord made me wait so long, He had a lot of molding to do with me. No wonder the "molding process" hurt so much –I was resisting every step of the way. I was so bitter that I got sent to the enemy's camp or Satan was allowed to capture me for a season, but the Lord knew I had to learn **II Corinthians 7:9b** for myself. Godly sorrow does lead to repentance. The problem is the church doesn't want to get near a man who has fallen spiritually. It's like when you were a kid and someone had 'cooties,' you didn't get near that person. The Lord knew all along that I could not look to the body of Christ where I grew up. There like much of the nation, many Christians are bleeding themselves profusely; they just refuse to see it. As bitter as I was towards so called "Christians" for "letting me down," I was just as guilty of my own sins blocked by the dark bitterness that so beset me!

I sat my family down one day, and told them things are very bad, but as Dad goes back to Christ so things will continue to improve in our quality of life. Believe me, The Lord never minds us taking some rest and relaxation.

Heavy emphasis on the word "some." I decided to start being <u>obedient</u> to the Lord and was able to improve little by little. When I desperately needed His divine intervention, God kept me humble because I was determined to obey His will.

> *Indeed it was for my own peace that I had great bitterness; but You have lovingly delivered my soul from the pit of corruption, You have cast all my sins behind Your back.* **Isaiah 38:17**

So, like the soldier who gets word he's going back to battle, I decided to polish up on the little things the Lord wanted me to clean up. Little things? My past incidents of road rage were a direct reflection of my inability to hold my temper. Going on 51 now, I can no longer pass my "hot temper" off on my Italian heritage. It's only been a few short years but for the most part – and of course with the Lord's help – I seem to have a handle on what used to be an uncontrollable temper. The more I bring my life in line with the Cross of Christ, the better things go for me. When I mess up (and I do), I can unequivocally point to the fact that the object of my faith and my attention has drifted proportionally away from the Cross! The sinful nature affects everyone! If you don't think it can happen to you, I hope you are right. My guess is you may be in trouble spiritually if you think that way.

Think you can't drift?

10 warning signs that you have drifted:
1. The way you act at church is different than you do at home. *You do or say things in the "world" that you would not do or say at church.*
2. You don't listen to people and rarely, if ever, take their advice.
3. Your foundational desire is not obedience to God.

4. You usually have the best answer for the question most of the time.
5. You think your way is always better.
6. You have a nagging sin habit you can't kick.
7. You are committing sins you once felt guilty for but now have desensitized yourself to it.
8. Every once in awhile God taps you on the shoulder for something you consider "minor" yet if it came down to losing a family member over it, you would drop to your knees in a public square and beg God for mercy if he would just save your family member or loved one.
9. You won't seek help because there is nobody you trust or who is smart enough to help you.
10. You are a guy and you look in the mirror more than 3 times a day ☺.

Jesus said, "...you must be born again"
As I said earlier in the book, the first step to getting back, in my opinion, to being "rescued," is taking a hard, TRUTHFUL look at yourself. Are you a seeker of TRUTH? Again, before you answer that, keep in mind, there will be a test! 80% of the world's population would tell you they **are** "Seekers of Truth." Using God and the Bible as my standard, I can assure you that 95% of them are WRONG! It always cracks me up when atheists try to convince us: "There is no God." How do they know? If it is true that "there is no God" then why do atheists fight so hard against something they say DOES NOT EXIST?

Furthermore, if God (as I know Him) is EVERYWHERE, can you name a single atheist that has been EVERYWERE? No, atheists are not Seekers of Truth. If you expect God to bless you and help you with your problems, you must become a Seeker of TRUTH .Let's move on

Jesus made an amazing statement about Himself. He said, *I am the TRUTH.* **John 14:6**

That's an astonishing statement for any man to make. I am the TRUTH? OK, what in the world does that mean? It means that when the universe was designed, Jesus was there. It means He really was born of a virgin, all a part of God's plan, formed eons ago or as recently as 6000 years ago – I know not when. That same plan included Jesus living for 33 and half years on this earth, only spending three and a half years teaching us EVERYTHING we need to know about life. It means He actually lived a life without sin, so that when His sacrificial death (just as God had planned it) came about, He and He alone could look at God and trade His life of perfection for our life of sinfulness and wrongdoing! It means that Jesus was either a liar or He was telling the truth about Himself. As I said, in order to be "rescued" you must be a TRUTH SEEKER at all levels of your life, including your personal inner-thoughts. In my case I was fooling myself, however, if you see yourself as a truth seeker, just know that one day, THE TRUTH is going to be standing above you while you are down on one knee, and He will judge how much you were a seeker of Truth. **Romans 14:11**

> *Whoever will save his life shall lose it.*
> **Matthew 16:25**

Allow me to address the longest problem with the shortest answer. If it has not been made clear to you by now, let me say it plainly. I would never be even a fraction of the man I am today, with all my shortcomings and all of my mistakes, had it not been for the "hard-times." I got healed because I started seeking God in truth, privately, but sincerely:

Hebrews 2:1: *Therefore we must give all the more attention* (heed) *to the things we have heard* (learned), *lest we drift away.*

Your "tiny little sin" – your "little secret sin(s)" – are holding you back from being healed completely and totally. That's right, it is only a tiny rudder that steers a big ship. You have to start to clean up your act before God sooner or later; you might as well start small, but START! Remember, baby steps start Trusting God in spirit and in truth. When it comes to that "tiny little sin" ask yourself – or as Jesus said, "Count the cost" – do you need to hang on to this so badly that you are willing to lose a loved one over it? I pray the answer is "NO!"

But your sins have separated between you and your God, and your sins have hid his face from you, that he will not hear. **Isaiah 59:2**

You need to start paying attention to that still small voice and realize that Jesus died for that specific sin in your life. Set your focus on the Cross.

The average prisoner where I was in county jail was of average intelligence or above. I encountered a low percentage of lower intelligence individuals although these individuals are represented on every block. These same guys do not (for the most part) have college degrees, but they are street smart. They know more about the law and appeals than many lawyers do. They also know when "authorities" bend and twist rules of procedure to get them convicted. In short, 98% of them feel the government is corrupt and the message of guys like Tim McVeigh is the type of message that resounds with them. Part of the devastating results of the sin of "pride" is that. not only do you not know you have it – it is the most deceiving of all sins – you actually think you are better than most people you associate with.

You can see how politicians and local officials get drunk with the power they have over people's rights. Our system of checks and balances is already out of whack. With the Supreme Court relying more on international law than it does the Constitution of the United States, it is just a matter of time before our nation's sovereignty gives way to global-ism and a one world government. This of course will wipe out over 200 years of history and make the sacrifices of those who laid down their lives for the cause of freedom and liberty, null and void.

People who are locked up these days see what I experienced firsthand and the very same authorities that I so proudly served. The same ones who are charged with upholding the laws and the RULES of PROCEDURE are the same ones I saw breaking their own rules time after time during my tenure as a police officer. The end justifies the means. In the United States, far fewer politicians are "Seekers of Truth" and it is the main reason our Government is out of whack. Those in authority in Washington are not "Truth Seekers".

SEARCH WARRANTS by police
In it is very rare in this country for judges to deny the police a "search warrant". The theory is that a judge must believe the officers are acting in "good faith" and indeed many do. However, there are growing number of law enforcement officers both at the local and Federal level who do not act in "good faith" but rather from a "the end justifies the means" mentality. The many in law enforcement today are driven by no other motive then the belief that they are the good guys therefore any and all opposition to their zeal must have as it's origin, a "bad-

guy". Judges on the other hand know that specific elements of a search warrant can be challenged in court, and therefore they are less inclined to deny a search warrant no matter how frivolous or weak the "probable cause" is for securing the warrant in the first place. Many search warrants today especially for drugs or ANYTHING remotely related to National security are obtained after much time (perhaps hours or days in some extreme cases) – the drugs or whatever is happened upon in a manner not consistent with the letter of the law. Most cops also worry (or believe) one technicality in a search warrant will bounce their case from court, it's a pride, I gotta win thing. They will deliberately create an entirely new set of circumstances so they can claim whatever contraband may have been found was in fact found. The police know from experience that a technicality can lose their case. In their mind putting this "scumbag" away becomes more important than playing by the very same rules they are supposed to uphold. Unfortunately, this behavior is not limited to "bending the rules", sometimes sworn police officers out-right lie! The Patriot Act implemented right after 9-11 has only exacerbated this problem.

Look at politicians today verses those of our Founding Fathers or even just 50 short years ago. How many portraits are there of George Washington on his knees, submitting to a "Higher Authority". President Lincoln pictured with his hand on the bible. President Truman having the courage to do what was in the countries best interest in spite of the plethora of criticism he endured. When was the last time you saw a modern politician "kneel" to anything, much less a sovereign God. Until just recently, the highest calling one could have in this great Nation of ours was God and Country. We are now living in a time when most of our politicians are dedicated to nothing more than getting re-elected and personal gain.

This is exactly why so many listeners of my talk radio show were so adamantly opposed to the Patriot Act. This is also why in my short tenure as a conservative spokesperson in Tucson, Arizona, I made it a point to go after the "liars" in government every chance I got.

Initially, I was in favor of the Patriot Act and told my listening audience that I would remain a "supporter" unless or until I saw Government Agents abuse the power we gave them. I've seen enough first hand Government abuse of power lately to know, we must get back many of our civil liberties before it is too late. On Friday March 9, 2007 a Justice Department audit concluded FBI abuse of the Patriot Act and I'm sure that was just the tip of the iceberg. For years, long before I had a radio show, I had been concerned about the "para-militarizing" of the police and its potential to create a "police state." We currently have laws on the books that do not allow our "military" to enforce domestic law. However, local Police departments are becoming so militarily trained and equipped these days, there is not much distinction between the two. One member of my listening audience wrote: Corrupt judges and Police Review Boards that get away with trampling American rights in the name of No-Knock Raids...which the current Supreme Court has ruled do not NEED to pause between screaming 'police.'" Police will now be busting in to flash-bang a family, slaughter the dog, and probably kill the homeowner as he attempts to defend himself! Winston Churchill is commonly credited with having said, "Democracy means that when there's a knock in the door at 3 am, it's probably the milkman."

Recently, R. Jeffrey Smith of the *Washington Post* wrote an article titled **White House Proposal Would Expand Authority of Military Courts** August 2, 2006.

In the article Mr. Smith reported: *A draft Bush administration plan for special military courts seeks to expand the reach and authority of such "commissions" to include trials, for the first time, of people who are not members of al-Qaeda or the Taliban and are not directly involved in acts of international terrorism, according to officials familiar with the proposal.*

As I told a friend of mine, what better way to start bringing modern day Minutemen to trial? Recently in Arizona, a State Representative named. Kyrsten Sinema authored a bill that would have tagged all Minuteman as "domestic terrorists". Modern day Minutemen around the country are doing nothing more then being a "neighborhood watch" at the border, and reporting illegal border crossers to the proper authorities. I'm pleased to report (to my knowledge) I am the only HONORARY MINUTEMAN in the country, so dubbed by Minuteman founder, Chris Simcox. Currently, Ms. Sinema is staging "seminars" with the help of the Mesa Arizona Police force, calling all who disagree with her about illegal immigration, "racists" and "white supremacists".

We are already seeing too many cases of Border Patrol agents being prosecuted on flimsy evidence, simply for doing their job! The idea that the **Department of Homeland Security** has prosecuted Border Patrol agents is a very scary turn indeed. Minuteman founder, Chris Simcox was prosecuted in this flimsy, 'get him any way you can' manner. It will not stop there! Another resident of Arizona, Casey Nethercutt, was also "railroaded" on the 'say-so' of an illegal alien. In a most treasonous manner, the judge in his case awarded the "victims" (two illegal's from Guatemala) his family ranch in Arizona!

I am very concerned that when the next terror attack takes place in the United States, those of us who want to protect and defend our country will be the subject of more government scrutiny, investigation, and prosecution than those who do the actual attacking. It's the nature of this "beast" we call government bureaucracy. They will spend more time constricting and restricting American citizens then they will fighting the actual terrorists. By all accounts, the United States will be attacked again and perhaps in ways that will make 9-11 pale in comparison.

"I am genuinely afraid that this political system (of ours), will not react until we lose a city! Nobody in this Country has thought about the threat to our civil liberties, the morning after we decide it's that dangerous, and how rapidly we will impose ruthlessness on ourselves in that kind of world. I think those of you who care about civil liberties had better be thinking through how we win this war (on terror), before the casualties get so great that the American people voluntarily give up a lot of those liberties." **Former Speaker of the House; Newt Gingrich**

At my trial, I recognized some of the same misdeeds and dirty tricks I used to use to get convictions. The local police detective and District Attorney defied many rules of evidence and procedure – similar to what I used to do – just so they could get me convicted. Lest you think I am judgmental, angry, and bitter, you are right, I was! Nevertheless, I am thankful today that the Lord cared enough about me to let me learn one of the fundamental lessons we need in serving Christ, **FORGIVENESS!** Once again, it is not a suggestion; it's a command of the Lord. **Matt 18:35**

I am grateful the Lord used "unsaved" people to dish out my punishment. The "after punishment" dished out by "Christians" was often much worse! Our jails are filling up with angry young men who need to hear the good news about Christ – He is all in all. He is everywhere at all times and He literally has it all under control. No need to kill abortion doctors, no need to blow up federal buildings. No need for your survival training, this is a war that is won at the foot of the cross, with the spoken WORD, love, and prayer.

As appalling as we find suicide bombers, nobody can say these young men and women are not dedicated to their cause. I bring this up only to compare the Christian response to tragedy in all too many sad incidents. How many of us even vote? That is a disgrace in and of it-self. The whole five years Deborah and suffered at the hands of our tormentors, I am sad to say we never voted one time that I can remember. My anger at the government was profound at that time. I am over it now because of the work of the Holy Spirit in me. I do not condone acts of "violence" to prove a cause. Thomas Jefferson said; *The tree of liberty must be refreshed from time to time with the blood of patriots and tyrants.* It is my prayer that the Lord will return before we reach a point in this Country, when that tree needs to be "refreshed." Some would suggest, it already needs refreshing. I do not agree. I do not agree with killing babies in the womb and I do not think anybody should kill doctors who perform abortions. I am not entirely in favor of capital punishment anymore either.

Take the case of Kirk Bloodsworth – a decorated former Marine from Maryland. Kirk was falsely accused of raping and killing a 9-year-old girl. As the judge pronounced Kirk's sentence – "DEATH BY LETHAL INJECTION" – the crowd erupted in gigantic applause and Kirk began seven years on death row, waiting for the state to legally end his life. The entire time he knew he never hurt that little girl. Kirk talks often about his time on "death row" – how vividly he remembers the hollering, screaming, and the awful smells that go with prison life. DNA later proved Kirk Bloodsworth's innocence. I am sure he thanks the Lord every day for his freedom. As of this writing there have been over 187 men released from death row because of DNA findings. When my past was used against me to try and hurt congressional candidate Randy Graf, I was asked by a reporter if I saw things differently since getting out of jail. I suppose the biggest change in my opinion of things is about the death penalty. I now believe the threshold for capital punishment should be higher than "reasonable doubt" – it should be "**no doubt!**"

There is something to be said for being willing to die for what you believe in. We see the reality of that in homicide bombers in the Middle East. I wonder how long it will be before a homicide bomber acts on U.S. soil? Regardless, Jesus requires nothing short of us to be willing to die as HE did. The good news is He does not require many of us to die physically, but He does require all of us to die spiritually. Dying to self is a Biblical teaching seldom heard from pulpits anymore. To be a true soldier in the army of God, a true Christian, you must be willing to die for what you believe in. With a government that slaughtered some 27 innocent children at WACO and nobody was held accountable. Watching the same government kill an innocent woman and baby at Ruby Ridge has filled many with rage and with contempt. The ever intrusive Government is trying harder every day to take God's place! There is only room for One God on the thrown of your life and it is NOT the Government!

Chapter 14
THE CABOOSE

Perhaps now you have a glimpse at God's eternal purpose for your life? What is that? "NO," you say? Start simple: If you were to die today and God asked you why He should allow you into Heaven, what would your answer be? If your answer is anything other than: *Because I accepted Christ's sacrificial death for me and I made Jesus my personal Savior,* then (according to the Bible) you are in trouble! For me it was the fact that the Bible has never been proven wrong! That makes the Bible a good bet at any odds. No matter how much "good" you do in life it can never meet God's standard and it's by grace we are saved not by "works," so nobody can truthfully say he *earned it*! If you have already made Jesus your personal Savior then take a look at that tiny little sin you refuse to let go of. To you it weighs less than an ounce; to God it weighs two million pounds! There is a bumper sticker philosophy out there that says; *I'm ok you're ok.* Now, should I believe a bumper sticker or God? Sorry, I'm going to bet my money on God. So, if it is TRUE that you do have a secret sin, you don't have to tell me or any person about it. Just get it right with God! If you are still confused, try reading and re-reading Romans Chapter 10, verses 10 and 11: you will get it.

As I mentioned earlier, I believe the Nation of Israel is the barometer of the world. I am also convinced that soon China will invade Taiwan, perhaps Japan. The Chinese army will march on Taiwan some day soon probably without firing a shot. In September of 2006 it was reported that China has been secretly firing laser beams to disable American satellites. What better way to keep us from watching the massive movement of troops that China will eventually use to threaten the free world. After our experience in Iraq, I seriously doubt that the United States has the belly to defend Israel when it is finally attacked again, much less come to the rescue of Taiwan when the Chinese decide to invade.

While we have been asleep at the wheel, China has amassed perhaps the largest military in the history of the world! China's blatant spying on the U.S. is well known; their demonstrated ability to shoot down space satellites got barely a "yawn" in the mainstream press. Yet our globalist politicians think nothing of it or the current trade deficit we have with this "most favored nation". The amount of money the United States owes China outright is astonishing. As I finish this book, China has made the United States of America impotent in many ways. China may soon realize its goal of becoming the world's only superpower. The good news about China? It appears the underground, Christian Church, has been growing simultaneously. Some estimate that there are as many as 200 million Christians in China.

Although my personal hope rests in God and God alone, I think about things like Asteroid's **2003 QQ47** – an asteroid that in the year 2014 could possibly strike the earth. It was amazing to me how that when Asteroid 2003 QQ47 was first discovered the "experts" said it only had a one in ten million chance of striking our planet. A few weeks later those chances were increased to one in five million and then the last I read, the "experts" are now upgrading the chances of hit hitting the earth to one in 900,000. Is it just me, or are the chances of that thing hitting us getting better? 2003 QQ47 is not the only one. There are many others with the potential to change life on earth as we know it, **1999 RQ36** or **2007 VK184.**

GOD DOES GOVERN IN THE AFFAIRS OF MEN!

I am concerned about the future of this great country of ours and its full speed ahead drive towards socialism. The new, false, religion of man made Global warming must rise as a stench in the nostrils of an Almighty and Jealous God! Even if the San Francisco court house one day is leveled by an act of God, those who drive the chariots full speed towards an eternity in hell will refuse to consider the obvious –

Already there is talk of requiring people to carry a biometric marker of some kind, a "chip" in your hand. Once again, is it just me, or are there correlations between these events and Bible predictions written over 2000 years ago?

666

And he causeth all, both small and great, rich and poor, free and bond, to receive a mark in their right hand, or in their foreheads:

And that no man might buy or sell, save he that had the mark, or the name of the beast, or the number of his name.

Here is wisdom. Let him that hath understanding count the number of the beast: for it is the number of a man; and his number is Six hundred threescore and six. **Revelation 13:16-18**

These things (when they happen) are only signs. Don't think for a second I am sitting around wringing my hands worrying about such things – I'm not and neither should you. To the believer the "earth is Lord's." **Psalm 24**

I can't help but wonder if Asteroid **2007 VK184** given a 1-in-2,940 chance of hitting the earth on 6-3-2048 – or Apophis, formerly known as Asteroid **2004 MN4**, might be the one talked about in Revelation, the one called "Wormwood"? **Revelation 8:10-13**

Then I read Isaiah chapter 24 where the Bible talks about God making the earth empty waste, turning it upside down, and scattering abroad the inhabitants of the earth, and making the land utterly un-inhabitable. Once again, as a believer, I do not fear any of these things and I most certainly am not saying 2007 VK184 or Apophis is THE one, but the Bible has a 2000 year history of never being wrong. From everything I read, Apophis **will strike the earth on April 13, 2029 or seven years later on April 13, 2036**. I don't think it is a coincidence that on March 24, 2007 European astronomers announced the discovery of Gliese 581c, commonly being called the "new earth". Again, I am not saying this is THE planet described in Revelation chapter 21, but it does give me optimistic pause. After about 2000 years of prophetic drought, 1948 and Israel becoming a nation again, was the super prophetic sign that seems to have ushered in many other bible prophecies. Eventually, all prophesy of the Bible will take place. Our assignment from God is simple, either get ready or help others to get ready. **Prov29:2**

Yes we are at war, but it is a spiritual war that must be fought for the hearts of men to desire good and not evil. Without that total commitment to the God of the Bible, we rob ourselves of so much blessing! Serving in the army of God brings joy where there is sadness, brings hope when there is only despair. Many of you have felt those feelings at one time, but now you forget where they are found. Like I used to teach the teenagers in YouthQuest; it's just like the Wizard of Oz where Dorothy clicks her red shoes together and says "there's no place like home, there's no place like home." That's how close the Lord is to you right now, He's right there at your feet with a TOWEL!!!! How long are you going to make him wait?

Start Focusing Now!

Have you ever read an instruction manual for a burglar alarm system? Inevitably, there is a diagram that looks like a confused maze. That's how many of us feel when trying to get our lives straightened out.

It may be a different town, it may be different people, but the essence of the lesson never leaves the believer, HE wants us to LEARN HIS WAYS! Focus is not something that comes easily, it is a discipline. Can you be a good Christian and never fast a meal? Sure you can. Can you be a good Christian and not read your Bible daily? Of course you can. The list goes on and on but here's the crux of the matter. Fasting, prayer and Bible study are a few of the many disciplines that we can implement in our lives that will help sharpen our ability to FOCUS. They will help you to make sense of the maze you seem to be tangled in, **but they are NOT the answer!**

As I said earlier, the object of your focus, indeed the object of your FAITH, must be in the Cross of Jesus Christ! Once again, I am not talking about two wooden beams nailed together, or a tattoo on your arm, or a piece of jewelry hanging from your rear view mirror. I am talking about focusing on the reality of the life of Christ and His willingness to suffer for your sins. His obedience unto death at the cross, and the resurrection power found ONLY in Jesus Christ. **The object of your faith, the object of your focus, must be on the Cross and what Jesus did for you there, personally!**

The more you focus on the Cross, the more faith you place in the grace of God, the more strength you will find, by way of the Holy Spirit, to focus on the Lord's will for your life. We get off course, when we tend to apply disciplines in our lives, at church, at home, on the job, anywhere. *If I just read my bible enough, If I just pray more, if I just join a twelve step program, if I just read that book or go to that seminar*....NO, NO, a thousand times NO!

Although these things in and of themselves can be good, they become "works" they become "laws" to us. These man-made "works" or "laws," attempt to strip Almighty God of the Glory He deserves when he frees us. When we join the "purpose driven life", or a "twelve step" program, or any number of things WE can do. It shifts the focus of our healing from God, back to us, and ends up crediting us for the mighty works, <u>only HE can do in us</u>! If all these other "things" worked, why would Jesus have to die for our sanctification?

I have been crucified with Christ; it is no longer I who live, but Christ lives in me; and the life which I now live in the flesh I live by faith in the Son of God, who loved me and gave Himself for me. I do not set aside the grace of God; for <u>if righteousness comes through the law, then Christ died in vain</u>. **Galations2:20-21**

We get so comfortable with our sins; sometimes the discipline to rid ourselves of sin seems impossible. Sexual sins, including masturbation, bring that temporary "high" some will vehemently fight to preserve. If you are a man and want to take issue with my opinion, just please don't try to tell me your sins are not as bad as any others. That argument – "well I never killed anyone or robbed a bank" just does not hold Biblical water. The same "high" that a man experiences when he commits sexual sin is first cousin to ANY addictive behavior – drugs or whatever, that produces the dopamine effect in a person's brain. It's the adrenaline "rush" men get addicted to; the actual behavior is usually secondary.

I suppose the same holds true for women. It has only been in recent years that we have seen a dramatic rise in female teachers having sex with young male students. What is wrong with this picture? I am not qualified to give you a diagnostic explanation however, it certainly makes a statement on present day society. Needless to say, anything sexual (outside of marriage) is a very slippery slope that ends with pain and suffering. This is also at the core of the demand by radical homosexuals for the "right" to get married, but that is a topic for an entire other book.

Without being judgmental, let me assure you only the Lord can provide protection so that you do not fall into sexual traps. I don't care how you spin it; if a "real man" is using Internet or some type of pornography or masturbation, he is defrauding his wife. In many cases, it seriously jeopardizes the marriage. I am still amazed at how men try to defend the "right" to this particular sin. How often have you heard a man say "there's no harm in looking"? Yet Jesus himself said *"...That whosoever looketh on a woman to lust after her hath committed adultery with her already in his heart."* Matt:5:28

Just because you do not see the harm in these sins does not mean they are not there. Discipline and focus are required to rid one-self of ALL sinful habits. That "discipline" comes from surrendering yourself at the foot of the Cross. Whether we admit it publicly or not, ridding oneself of sinful habits is difficult. If it were easy, everyone would do it. Thousands of self-help books, ministries, twelve step programs, treatment centers, have been developed over the years. Without Step one of those programs, without a determination and discipline, those programs become nothing more than a "reed shaken in the wind". NOTHING can take place of God's GRACE. "Determination" and "discipline" to do God's will, will always receive God's help in time of need. When we learn the nature of God, we find that none of us is worthy. However, when we learn the true meaning of "grace" to the true Christian it is not a matter of being "good" it becomes a daily struggle to do better! This can only be accomplished by making the Cross of Christ the object of our faith! Too many people think the concept of Salvation by Grace is just too simple. That is why so many people give up and give in. How nice would church life be if we actually helped each other with our weaknesses instead of trying to devour one another? How nice it would be if we were not an Army that shoots its own wounded! Time to think about going it alone, just you and the Lord.

God does test us, <u>he does not tempt us,</u> but He does test us. Once you have passed God's test, you are ready to move on to the next level with the Lord, whatever HE has in store for you. All this makes the promise of the Lord come to light... *"His lord said unto him, Well done, thou good and faithful servant: thou hast been faithful over a few things, I will make thee ruler over many things: enter thou into the joy of thy lord. . '* **Matthew 25:21 (KJV)**

You may be asking yourself at this point – how do I learn to focus? Good question! I won't say that it has been an easy discipline for me to learn and please don't think I have all the answers, none of us do. Keep in mind; sinless perfection is only a goal. Sinless perfection is an illusion to the man or woman who thinks they have finally achieved it. Sinless perfection cannot be had on this side of heaven. I would like to share with you three things that the Lord has taught me on focusing. These truths learned in the midst of trials have helped me to redirect my focus from myself, or circumstances, or other people, and put it back on where it should be, on the Cross of Jesus Christ!

KEEP YOUR EYES ON JESUS!

At one time Rome and its Caesar(s) ruled the entire known world. The Roman Empire would conquer a country somewhere around the world and meet with token resistance. Nobody in those days had "battle tactics" like the Empire did. It was well organized, FOCUSED. Its focus was so great that young boys grew up with no other purpose in life than to serve Rome. Roman generals were basically rated on how many foreign countries they conquered and the Roman armies were so far advanced in their weaponry that no one on the face of the earth could compete.

However, Rome made the same mistake we in the United States make today. Whether it is a successful society like the Roman Empire or you and I on an individual level, all of us have a preponderance to stray off course, to seek creature comforts, fleshly desires – a desire for the pleasures of life. Sadly, much of the Christian church has strayed from the cross of Jesus Christ! This should not be confused with having our own "happiness," for the Lord does desire that you be happy and content with your life. However, when those "desires" become our focus, when pursuing those desires grows in excess, it is then that we weaken and begin to fail.

From WW II until September 11 when the United States was defiled by terrorists at the World Trade Center and the Pentagon, we had little focus in this Country. The misplaced sixties mentality of "peace and love" replaced a Christian perspective for many or in some cases, good old-fashioned common sense. We had taken our sights off the goals upon which our great country was originally established, individual freedom and liberty. Our forefathers were not trying to establish a country with freedom FROM religion but one with freedom OF religion. A religion based on a relationship is not a "form" or established government church. Government will never be able to establish a freedom FROM religion. When tragedy strikes like the initial WTC attack, the first thing that stirs in the hearts of the people is to pray, to FOCUS spiritually.

Soup kitchens, halfway houses, drug and alcohol treatment centers and a host of other "human services" have their roots in religion. Religion is not the "opiate of the people" as Karl Marx once proclaimed. It gives society FOCUS. It allows even the "least among us" to find the Lord, because it bends people's hearts toward God.

CONCENTRATE ON DOING ONE THING AT A TIME!

Then Peter, turning around, saw the disciple whom Jesus loved following, who also had leaned on His breast at supper, and said, Lord, which is he that betrayeth thee? Peter seeing him saith to Jesus, Lord, and what shall this man do? Jesus saith unto him, If I will that he tarry till I come, what is that to thee? follow thou me **John 21:20-22.**

As I said earlier, too often we worry about what everyone else is doing or why God blesses THEM and not us. While Jesus is telling us, just as he told Peter when he worried about what was going to happen to John, *"If I will that he tarry till I come, what is that to thee? follow thou me."*

In other words, mind your own business!

In order for us to stay focused, we must stop comparing ourselves to other people, ministries, or churches. If you find yourself in a fallen or defeated state, get up. Find that one thing the Lord may be urging you to change. It may be a sin, an unhealthy practice, an emotional change. Maybe you are hanging with the wrong crowd. The list goes on and on – but take charge of that one thing. Apply your focus about that "thing" to the Cross of Christ and nothing else. Ask the Lord to help you with it and stay at the foot of the Cross until HE frees you, HE WILL!

Even though I buried my life in racquetball at one point, as the Lord began to show me how much of my time and efforts were being wasted, I slowly loosened my grip on the sport and the close associations I had developed. I prayed a lot and was bold-faced honest with God. I actually was brazen enough to say to God: "ok, I'll give up racquetball but what are you going to do for me?" How dumb was that?

The Lord loves us so much, He even tolerates our foolish pompous ways (to an extent). I sure don't recommend dealing with God like that, but what did I have to lose? I was enjoying the party life so much, yet all the while I knew I needed/wanted to be back in a right relationship with God. So, probably as flippantly as I ever had, I acted like I was calling the shots and "dared" God to bless me if I kept my end of the deal. Almost everyone I know who ever made a "deal" with God ended up not keeping his or her end of the bargain. I know I did the same years ago but I was determined not to repeat the same mistake. Remember my circle theory? Well, God blessed me indeed. The more HE blessed me, the more I began to grow spiritually. How immature is that, you might ask? Believe me, when I was so wrapped in my own self-righteousness, I would have asked the same thing.

Let me see if I can put it in perspective for you. If you are dying in the desert as I was – spiritually speaking, I was famished in this deserted place for years. I wrote God a letter once, a portion of which went like this: *I'm dying, I don't see you anywhere God. I pray it seems like you don't hear me. I go to 'Christian' leaders and 'friends' and I get nothing, no rescue, no words of encouragement it's more like people in churches can't run from me fast enough, I'm dying! If you just get me out of this deserted place I'll change, I'll straighten up, or whatever it is you think I need to do.* God did not get me out of the desert, but He did make it rain! I must tell you, I danced for joy in that rain. <u>He will do the same for you!</u>

People around me like Pastor Tim Smoyer and a handful of others began to see the new life emerging from me again. Even though HE did not remove me from that place, He did send me a Red Cross package. Just the fact that the Lord took the time to send me a response was good enough for me. The more I responded, the more He communicated; the more He communicated, the more I responded. He WILL do the same for you! Finally, my relationship with the Lord started to resemble the way it should have been all along. That is my prayer for you! This time He has burned so much of the impurities away, I see clearer now than I ever did. No more being a phony or a hypocrite, I am the man God made me to be, including my "screw-up's". I only pray He never stops teaching me. The more we respond, the more He "enlarges our coasts." Before you know it soldier, you are back in the game and God is going to use you to accomplish mighty things!

A case in point is a testimony by a minister named, Rev. Joe Wright. I do not know a thing about Rev. Wright except this: He was asked to give the opening prayer in

Kansas at the opening session of their Senate, January 23, 1996. I remember the first time one of my books was quoted in the Pennsylvania House of Representatives. I was so thrilled! I can't imagine how far I would have missed God had I been in Rev. Wright's place. You may have read on the Internet how Pastor Wright was asked to open the new session of the Kansas Senate and he used the opportunity that the Lord had opened to Him and focused on doing that one thing to the best of his ability. Everyone was expecting the usual generalities, but this is what they heard:

Heavenly Father, we come before you today to ask your forgiveness and to seek your direction and guidance. We know Your Word says, Woe to those who call evil, good," but that is exactly what we have done. We have lost our spiritual equilibrium and reversed our values. We confess that we have ridiculed the absolute truth of Your Word and called it Pluralism. We have exploited the poor and called it the lottery. We have rewarded laziness and called it welfare. We have killed our unborn and called it choice. We have shot abortionists and called it justifiable. We have neglected to discipline our children and called it building self-esteem. We have abused power and called it politics. We have coveted our neighbor's possessions and called it ambition. We have polluted the air with profanity and pornography and called it freedom of statement. We have ridiculed the time-honored values of our forefathers and called it enlightenment.

Search us, Oh, God, and know our hearts today; cleanse us from every sin and set us free. Guide and bless these men and women who have been sent to direct us to the center of Your Will and to openly ask these things in the name of Your Son, the living Savior, Jesus Christ. Amen!"

Like an idiot back then, I probably would have hired a PR firm, had my own photographer cover the event and used it as a fundraiser in my next newsletter. God had the right man for the job in Rev. Wright. Believe me; he did not make many friends that day. It was reported that the response was immediate. A number of legislators walked out during the prayer in protest. In six short weeks, Central Christian Church, where Rev. Wright is pastor, logged more than 5,000 phone calls with only 47 of those calls responding negatively. The church is now receiving international requests for copies of this prayer from India, Africa, and Korea.

There is no telling what God can do through you! Great victories are won when you do not let fear of failure or worry of what someone else is doing hold you back. You must train yourself to concentrate on getting your focus on the Cross of Christ not your ability. Keep doing that one thing until the Lord tells you otherwise, NEVER forget who blessed you with an opportunity.

REMEMBER YOUR TRAINING!!!!!!

As I said earlier, any self-defense trainer in the world will tell you – your TRAINING will determine how you react in any abrupt circumstance. If you have no training, chances are you will have no reaction (or the wrong one). If you train yourself, you will use your training instinctively for survival. When a soldier is in the midst of the battle, all he or she has to rely upon is what they have learned in their training. We as Christians are the same way. When we are in the heat of testing, trials or tribulation, it is what we have learned of the Lord that will sustain us through these times. God is famous for giving us the test first, THEN teaching us the lesson(s). Our strength does not come from taking a stand, it actually comes from taking a knee. We cannot control many things that happen to us, but we can control how we react to them. Our ability to focus is strongly linked to how diligently we have been in our training.

I have no intention of backing down from what I believe is the truth of God's word and what will ultimately help bring men and women to Christ. Regardless of what they say about me, I am not the issue! I am not the story, try as they might. The Lord has shown me that if I stay focused, no weapon formed against me will prosper! **Isaiah 54:17**

How is your focus? Are you disciplining yourself? Are you keeping your eye on Christ and Him crucified for you? Are you concentrating on trying to do your best to accomplish one thing at a time and do it well? Finally, are you remembering your training? If not, go back and do the things you did at first to reestablish that foundation. Until you do, your FOCUS will be out of alignment. God's plan is for us to focus on His plan and keep the Cross of Christ at the forefront of our lives, our homes and our ministries!

I don't know why I have been given the opportunity to learn from so many great Christian leaders of our nation. I just know that over the years the Lord put me in places, with people I never dreamed possible to meet. I am determined not allow any level of "success" get to my head again. This is why I so enjoyed my work as a lobbyist in Washington, D.C. in spite of the horrific ending we had. I counted it a privilege to learn from good, Christian, Congressmen, Senators, leaders, and staff. Many of them have a lot on the ball, but they have personal struggles just like you!

No matter what position you hold in the "Army of God" you are going to have struggles with evil!!!! It's the way things work around here. Why do you think Jesus said "…and lead us NOT into temptation…" we are all tempted!

Don't ever look at another person and think they are worthless! We are ALL sinners according to the Word of GOD! In comparison to the Holiness and righteousness of God, we all are stained with sin. The Bible says even our righteousness is as "filthy rags" compared to God. **Isaiah. 64:6**

Put simply, we are saved by Grace alone, it is important to read your bible, pray, and get back to church. However, it is only the sacrificial blood of Christ and the grace of God that sets people free. Start leading others to a relationship with God, or help a wounded soldier back on his or her feet. If by teaching you the things I have learned, you become a soldier in the army of God again, or you sign up for the very first time, I have done what I have been called to do.

My family paid a horrible price for my sins; you may be going through similar circumstances. As for me, I am back now for good! I would be remiss if I did not thank my current Pastors; Bruce Brock and Adrian Suarez. These men thought enough of me and knew enough of the amazing grace of God, to ordain me a "Pastor" again. Waiting to hear those immortal words; *Well done thou good and faithful servant!*

Hang in there! It does get better! Now GO!

The end!

"forgetting those things which are behind, and reaching forth unto those things which are before I press toward the mark for the prize of the high calling of God in Christ Jesus"
Phil.3:13-14.

Thanks to **Deborah Prihoda** for her help and contributions. Extra special "thanks" to **Liudyte Baker**, without whose help this project may never have been finished.

Cover and design by Sarah Aiken & Stephanie Miramontes
Also **THANK YOU** to the "very few" *mentioned on page 23*, who stood by us and who are not specifically mentioned in this book: Renn & Marian, Steve & Kathy, John & Heather, David, Sheila, Denise & Bruce, John & Nancy, Doug & Regina

Deborah, Mindy, Sarah, and Steph: With all my screw-ups, I just want to say, I love you guys more than you will ever know! Thank you for forgiving me. Love, Dad
Philippians 2:12

Dear Micah,
12/25/2005
The things I do, I do, for the Lord, for you and your brothers and sisters and cousins who will follow!
May you grow up to be a WARRIOR for God and may you learn from your Heavenly Father! Do Justly, love mercy, and walk humbly with God!
Love,
pop-pop

Copyright 2006 Steve Aiken
www.steveaiken.com